What Life Was Like®

IN THE TIME OF WAR AND PEACE

Imperial Russia
AD 1696 ~ 1917

What Life Was Like

IN THE TIME OF WAR AND PEACE

Imperial Russia
AD 1696 ~ 1917

BY THE EDITORS OF TIME-LIFE BOOKS, ALEXANDRIA, VIRGINIA

CONTENTS

IN THE TIME OF
WAR AND PEACE

THREE HUNDRED YEARS OF ROMANOV RULE

On July 11, 1613, a new tsar was crowned in the Cathedral of the Assumption in Moscow. His name was Mikhail Feodorovich, and great expectations were pinned on him. The fledgling Russian state had just gone through a 15-year period of foreign war and domestic upheaval known as the Time of Troubles, and it was hoped that 16-year-old Mikhail Feodorovich, or "son of Feodor," would lead Russia into better times. Among his chief assets was the link he provided with the country's glorious past. Mikhail III was a Romanov, a family related by marriage to the man considered the greatest of all Russian rulers, Ivan IV,

or as history would remember him, Ivan the Terrible.

Ivan IV was the first of the Russian tsars. He had come to power in the mid-16th century as the prince of Muscovy, a kingdom centered on Moscow and one among many then existing in the land of the people called the Rus. But Ivan was not satisfied to rule Muscovy alone. He declared himself *tsar*—a word derived from the Roman title *caesar*—and the rightful ruler of all Russia; he then set about conquering the neighboring principalities. He expanded his realm west toward the Baltic and east into Siberia, laying the foundation of his country's future as a great empire.

1547	1613	1695-1725	1700-1721
Ivan IV (the Terrible) adopts the title of "tsar." Reigned 1533-1584	Mikhail III (1613-1645) becomes the first Romanov tsar	Sole reign of Peter I (the Great)	The Great Northern War between Russia and Sweden

By the time he died in 1584, Ivan had established Russia as a unified state, one over which he had absolute—and tyrannical—power.

Ivan's successors, Mikhail III and the Romanov tsars that followed him, did lead Russia out of its Time of Troubles, and the dynasty would continue to rule the country for the next 304 years. But the leader most responsible for building on Ivan's imperial ambitions was Mikhail's grandson, the fourth of the Romanov tsars and the first to assume the title of emperor—Peter the Great.

The Russia that Peter inherited at the end of the 17th century was vast, overwhelmingly rural, and intensely religious. Untouched by Renaissance or Reformation, it was as much Eastern in outlook as Western, as two minded as the double-headed eagle that was the Romanov family em-

blem. To visitors from Europe it was a strange and mystical land, beautiful yet barbaric. And it was a land that Peter I was determined to change.

First, Peter expanded his borders by warring with the Turks, Persians, and Swedes. From Sweden he captured the Baltic coastline as far south as Riga, and on this coast Peter built a new capital, giving it the distinctly un-Russian name of St. Petersburg. Although Moscow remained an alternative capital, the transfer of the seat of government to St. Petersburg marked the end of old Muscovy and the beginning of the new Russia. It was a sign of what was to come.

With characteristic energy and determination, Peter embarked on a vigorous crusade to reform Russia internally in every possible way. He constructed roads and canals, built up the army and created a navy, redesigned the

1762-1796	1812	1861	1881
Reign of Catherine II (the Great), widow of Peter III	Napoleon invades Russia and takes Moscow but retreats before winning a Russian surrender	Alexander II (1855-1881) emancipates Russia's serfs, earning the title "Tsar-Liberator"	Alexander II is assassinated and is succeeded by his son, Alexander III

structure of the government, redefined the relationship between church and state, and directly spurred industrial, technological, and economic growth. By the time he died in 1725, the face of Russia had been changed forever.

For 37 years following Peter's death, Russia was governed by a half-dozen largely ineffectual emperors and empresses. It was not until 1762 that the country once again had a powerful and effective ruler. Her name was Sophia Augusta Fredericka, a princess from a tiny German principality who married into the Romanov family. Upon her conversion from Lutheranism to Russian Orthodoxy, she took the name Catherine, and like Peter, she would earn her title, "the Great."

Catherine had much in common with Peter. She was a strong and ambitious ruler who wanted Russia to be an outward-looking, world-class power. She was aggressive in foreign policy and succeeded in enlarging her realm significantly. And she devoted much energy to internal reforms, rebuilding more than 200 Russian towns, constructing roads between them, and founding schools based on modern educational theories.

But Catherine also differed from Peter. Although both rulers promoted Western ways, Peter's interest in the West was much more pragmatic than Catherine's. She was a product of European court life and fancied herself an "enlightened despot" and a cultural sophisticate. She made every effort to foster art, literature, architecture, music, and education in Russia. Over time, though, Catherine became more of a traditional Russian autocrat than an enlightened despot, especially once she came to realize that Enlighten-

1894	1904-1905	January 1905	August 1914
Alexander III dies and is succeeded by his son, Nicholas II, last of the Romanov tsars	The Russo-Japanese War	Bloody Sunday massacre in St. Petersburg sparks the 1905 Russian revolution	Russia enters World War I against Germany

ment philosophy did not translate easily into practical politics, particularly in Russia.

Of the emperors and empresses that followed Catherine, some were reformers, others reactionaries. But no matter who was in power, little changed for the vast majority of Russia's 45 million people. The European manners and customs of St. Petersburg and Moscow—home to less than one and a half percent of the population at the start of the 19th century—had little relevance to the rest of Russia, where the people remained deeply traditional in culture, religion, and social systems, tied to the land and the old ways of family, village, and church.

In 1894 Nicholas II ascended the throne. A devoted husband and indulgent father, he was more interested in family life than life at court. He was, however, determined to preserve the autocratic system of government, but he was singularly incapable of doing so. He was ill equipped to manage the turbulence of early-20th-century Russia, and his was a reign characterized by foreign wars, social alienation, and revolution. When change did come, it swept Nicholas and his family away and so ended the rule of the Romanovs. The dynasty that had come to power in one time of troubles had perished in another.

In the chapters ahead we will consider what life was like in Romanov Russia, from the imperial reign of Peter the Great to the last days under Nicholas II. We will see life on the great country estates and in the growing cities, in Catherine the Great's Hermitage inside the Winter Palace, in peasant cottages, in the manor houses of the grandees, in church, in revolution, in war, and in peace.

March 1917

Nicholas II abdicates the throne, a provisional government is established, and the Russian imperial era ends

November 1917

Vladimir Lenin and the Bolsheviks overthrow Russia's provisional government; nationwide civil war ensues

July 1918

Nicholas II and his family are murdered

December 1922

Civil war ends and the USSR is officially born

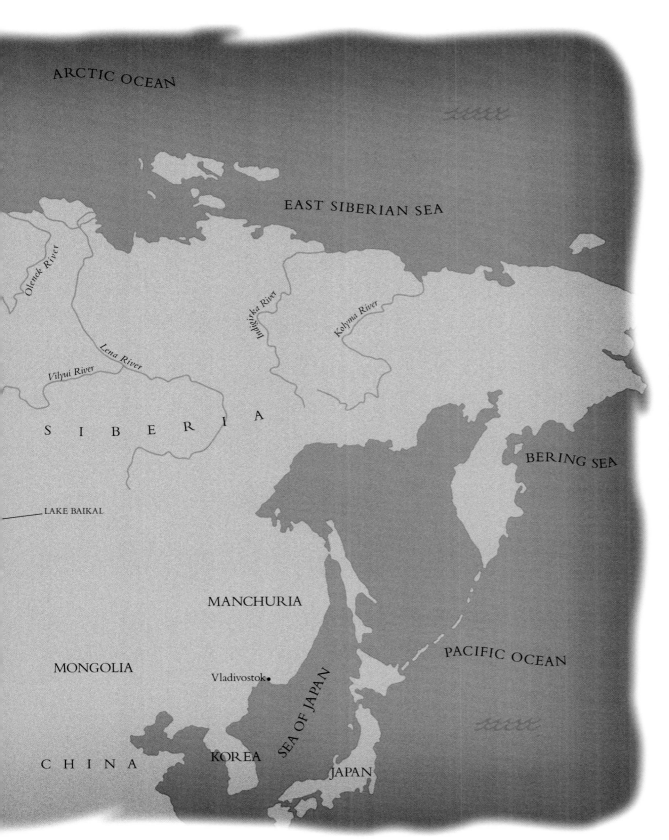

ARCTIC OCEAN

EAST SIBERIAN SEA

Olenek River

Indigirka River

Kolyma River

Lena River

Vilyui River

S I B E R I A

BERING SEA

LAKE BAIKAL

MANCHURIA

PACIFIC OCEAN

MONGOLIA

Vladivostok•

SEA OF JAPAN

C H I N A

KOREA

JAPAN

Larger in size than the Soviet state that replaced it, 19th-century imperial Russia covered fully one-sixth of the earth's surface, extending from the Baltic Sea in the west to the Bering Sea in the east and from the Arctic Ocean to central Asia. Most of the country is an enormous plain broken only by the Ural Mountains, the traditional boundary between Europe and Asia. Other mountain ranges rise around the edges of the plain, marking the borderlands of Russia: the Carpathians in the southwest, the Caucasus between the Black and Caspian Seas, and the mighty Asian ranges to the south.

But despite its vast size—some 5,000 miles from sea to sea—the heart of Russia has always been west of the Urals. It was there, in old Muscovy, that the state was born, and there, too, that Peter the Great founded the city of St. Petersburg—a port for his navy, a capital for his country, and Russia's "window on the West."

CHAPTER ONE

RUSSIA LOOKS TO THE WEST

Peter the Great, Russia's indomitable ruler at the beginning of the 18th century, was the first tsar also to be called emperor. Almost single-handedly, Peter transformed old Russia into a true empire that, by the time of his death, had become a major European power. Here he wears the star of the Order of St. Andrew, the apostle who is credited with bringing Christianity to Russia.

Under a scorching August sun in the shipyards of Amsterdam in 1697, a team of carpenters grunted and sweated to complete the construction of a 100-foot frigate. Among them was a vigorous young man they called Carpenter Peter. Twenty-five years old and bristling with energy, this so-called Peter Timmerman eagerly sought a new task the moment one was finished. A slim youth, he towered over his companions from a height of just under seven feet. His round, fine-featured countenance, with its alert eyes and small brown mustache, was marred slightly by a wart on the right cheek, and under emotional stress his face would break into a nervous twitch.

He was dressed in the same sort of clothes as his coworkers, sporting a red jacket over a collarless shirt with large buttons, white canvas knee breeches, and a cone-shaped felt hat. Peter's garments, however, did not show the stains and repairs of years of wear, as did those of the other workmen. An observer would have noticed, too, that the others were always a little more reserved when Peter was among them. For although they pretended otherwise, they knew his true identity: The seemingly humble young man was in fact the Tsar of All the Russias, who would one day be known as Peter the Great.

For five months, Peter Timmerman worked alongside the Dutch carpenters, who had been cautioned by their employers never to allow him to know they were privy to his secret. Each day at sunrise, Peter joined them, setting to work with an ax, plane, or adz. The ax, an observer noted, "he wields more skillfully than all the other carpenters there." Sometimes he simply helped carry the large beams for the body of the vessel. When the work exhausted him, he stopped for a few moments to rest on a log. Unlike his fellows, he often took the latter part of the day off for sailing or rowing.

There was, however, a serious purpose to Peter's masquerade. The young tsar had decided to tour Europe in the spring of 1697—incognito—in order to raise allies and garner western technical knowledge for Russia's war against the Turks. Some 250 Russians traveled on the 18-month-long "great embassy" to western Europe. Among them were 35 "volunteers" who would master such critical technical skills as carpentry, sailmaking, and mast building.

One of the volunteers was a sailor who called himself Peter Mikhailov, alias Peter Timmerman, secretly the young tsar. And while his disguise fooled no one, Peter's hosts went along with the game, thereby permitting the tsar to dispense with some of the formalities and protocol an official visit would entail.

As he progressed on his long journey, Peter visited museums, laboratories, botanical gardens, an anatomy class where he witnessed a dissection, and factories of every sort. Questioning both officials and workers, he took copious notes and measurements, and sometimes operated the factory machines himself. He learned how to pull teeth after watching a demonstration in a public square; procuring his own set of tools, Peter then practiced on those of his unfortunate companions whose teeth he thought needed treatment, sometimes pulling out bits of gum in the process. In the German port city of Königsberg, using the name Peter Mikhailov, he took artillery lessons from a colonel who gave him a certificate recognizing him as "an accomplished bombardier."

Peter charmed some of the aristocrats who entertained him on his journey. In Hanover, for example, early in his tour, he dined with the electress Sophia and her daughter. Sloppily scooping up his food with his fingers and dripping much of it on his clothes, he left Sophia wishing his manners were "a little less rustic." She nonetheless commended him, in a letter to a friend, for his "great vivacity of mind" and his "noble sentiments," noting that "he was very merry, very talkative."

Dinner in Hanover was followed by a ball, which divulged its own technical secrets: Upon

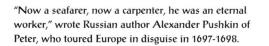

"Now a seafarer, now a carpenter, he was an eternal worker," wrote Russian author Alexander Pushkin of Peter, who toured Europe in disguise in 1697-1698.

taking hold of his dancing partner, Peter was astonished to feel her whalebone corset, an article of underclothing unknown in Russia. "These German ladies have devilish hard bones!" he blurted out. Even more surprised was a 10-year-old princess that Peter singled out for special attention: Grabbing her by the ears, he lifted her little face up to his in order to give her a kiss.

After leaving Holland, Peter sailed to England, where his hosts were somewhat less enchanted with him. In London, Peter and his men settled into a home loaned to him by an Englishman named John Evelyn. The house was located near the royal dockyards at Deptford, where he could study naval architecture. He also toured the Royal Greenwich Observatory, the Tower of London, and the houses of Parliament, noting in his journal: "It is good to hear subjects speaking truthfully and openly to their King. This is what we must learn from the English." What he failed to learn, however, was restraint. In the home of their host, Peter and his volunteers enjoyed numerous bouts of drunken merrymaking in their rough, uninhibited Muscovite fashion. They smashed furniture, tore curtains, splattered the walls and floors, stomped the lawn into mud, and used the portraits that hung on the walls for target practice. Evelyn was eventually granted £350 from the royal treasury for repairs.

Peter delighted in the cities and suburbs of London and Amsterdam, impressed by the number, size, and elegance of their stone-built buildings. Moscow, a large, overcrowded city of nearly 200,000 inhabitants, had as many as 40,000 houses. But in the Russian capital, rich and poor alike lived in dwellings built of logs, the poor in rows of humble huts, the nobles mostly in single-story villas with tiny windows. Both types of residences were frequently devastated by fires.

Five years after his trip abroad, Peter would begin to build St. Petersburg, a new imperial capital with well-planned, wide avenues, canals like those of Amsterdam, and houses constructed out of stone. And throughout his three-decade reign, Peter would institute dramatic changes that would catapult Russia from a backwater regime to the ranks of the highly respected European nations. But among his immediate successors, only one would also aspire to significant reform. This was Catherine II, who would captivate Europe and much of the world.

It was during Peter's extraordinary and at times terror-ridden childhood that his hunger for technical knowledge developed. His father, Alexei, had married Maria Miloslavskaya, who died in 1669, leaving the 40-year-old tsar six daughters and two sickly sons, Feodor and Ivan. Two years later, Alexei married again. He had fallen in love with a beautiful young noblewoman, Natalya Naryshkina, but allowed the traditional process of tsarist wife choosing to run its course.

As was customary, the loveliest young virgins of Russia were summoned to the Kremlin complex in Moscow, where ladies of the highest standing at court weeded out the least worthy among the candidates for tsarina. They did this by questioning them and also by examining and feeling every part of their undressed bodies to ensure the quality of their physical charms. Some were sent away, but those who qualified stood nervously waiting for the tsar to make his choice. Alexei walked among the young women, not to assess them as his predecessors had done, but to look for the person he had already selected. When at last he stood before Natalya, he offered her a gold-and-pearl-embroidered handkerchief. Her acceptance of the cloth completed their betrothal.

With Natalya came her family, the Naryshkins, to supplant the power and prestige of his first wife's kin, the Miloslavskys. And from then on, a fierce enmity simmered between the two clans. Natalya, to her husband's delight, in 1672 gave birth to a healthy, lively son named Peter, followed by two daughters. Three and a half years after Peter was born, Alexei died, leaving the 15-year-old Feodor to rule. Feodor was allied to his mother's family, the Miloslavskys, and so, with a vengeance, his maternal relatives swept the Naryshkins out of their high offices. Natalya and Peter went to live in a modest wooden villa at Preobrazhenskoe, a village just outside Moscow.

The new tsar, frequently ill, allowed his sister Sofia—four years his elder—to manage the affairs of state. While he languished, Feodor worried about who would succeed him. The choice lay between his retarded brother, Ivan, with Sofia as regent, and his popular half brother, Peter, with Natalya at the helm. When Feodor died in April 1682, Sofia moved to protect her position. She circulated rumors among the Moscow Streltsy—an official guard, 22 regiments strong—that the Naryshkins had poisoned Feodor and were planning to assassinate Ivan. Worked into a rage, the Streltsy marched to the Kremlin, stormed the palace, and killed any Naryshkin supporters they could find. Nevertheless, on May 26, Ivan and Peter were crowned as co-tsars. But Sofia, as regent, meant to rule Russia herself, and so Peter and his mother once again were banished to Preobrazhenskoe.

Had he been raised in the Kremlin, as were his forebears, Peter's days would have been planned for him and supervised by tutors, and any spontaneity or independence probably would have been stifled. In exile at the villa, however, he was able to devote himself to what interested him most. The athletic youngster abounded with energy and curiosity. From his tutor he learned to read and write, memorizing prayer- and psalmbooks and much of the New Testament. Peter supplemented this fairly rudimentary education with his own explorations. Intrigued by mechanical gadgets, he took them apart to discover how they worked. He loved carpentry and spent hours on woodworking projects.

At Preobrazhenskoe Peter was also able to choose his own companions. Many of the children and adults with whom he spent his time came from a nearby district known as the "German suburb." It was a measure of the Russian suspicion of outsiders that foreigners of all nationalities, some 1,500 of them in the 1680s, were restricted to living there. The inhabitants in-

cluded a wide variety of artisans, and the young tsar was eager to absorb their skills. Many of these craftsmen created furniture of European design, such as upholstered chairs, inlaid pedestal tables, and clocks, for the Russian gentry to add to their typical furnishings of wooden benches, chests, and long tables. Growing up among such foreigners, Peter failed to develop the traditional Russian enmity to outsiders. Instead, he acquired an egalitarian outlook, remarkable for a monarch.

When he was 16, Peter was given an astrolabe, an instrument used to determine the position of the sun and other heavenly bodies. Peter's search for someone who could explain how it worked led him to a Dutch merchant named Timmerman. Under Timmerman's tutelage, Peter began a serious study of mathematics and such military arts as ballistics and fortifications. He filled notebooks with problems that he solved in these subjects, but his writings were riddled with mistakes in grammar and spelling that reflected the poor quality of his early education.

One day, while exploring an old warehouse with Timmerman, Peter came upon a wreck of a boat. It was an English vessel with a deep, rounded hull and pointed bow that, according to Timmerman, was better than its flat-bottomed Russian counterpart. "Why is it better?" Peter demanded.

"Because it can sail with the wind and also against the wind," was Timmerman's answer.

Keen to try it out, Peter had one of the foreign carpenters replace the timbers and tar the hull. When the repairs were finished, Peter leaped into the boat, seized the tiller, and soon learned to tack with the wind. He delighted in sailing and in all aspects of navigation. Later he would call that small boat "the grandfather of the Russian navy."

Over the years, Sofia had remained aware of the danger that her half brother, Peter, posed to her reign. And when in 1689 Natalya chose a wife for her 17-year-old son, a woman of the

With his tutor, young Peter studies naval science and
fortification, subjects of lifelong interest. As tsar, he
commissioned Russia's first navy.

nobility named Eudoxia Lopukhina, Sofia decided it was time
for the Streltsy to take action on her behalf.

Shortly after midnight on August 7, 1689, Peter was awakened at the villa by two palace guardsmen loyal to his family.
They revealed that Sofia had, for 25 rubles apiece, bribed the
Streltsy to surround Peter's village the next night and murder all
who were part of his life—his mother, wife, servants, advisers,
and friends. Memories of the earlier Streltsy massacres overwhelmed Peter, who jumped out of bed, saddled a horse, and fled
into the forest, still in his nightshirt. After he had taken refuge
in a monastery, word was passed to his family and supporters,
who joined him within the sturdy walls of the holy place.

Eventually a number of Streltsy regiments and several other
military units marched to the monastery in support of Peter.
Her own military strength diminished, Sofia sent the patriarch
of the Orthodox Church to negotiate with Peter. But the clergyman joined Peter's forces, too. Finally she decided that she
would reason with her half brother herself and rode off to the
monastery. At its gates, however, she was informed that he would
not see her. Left with few supporters, Sofia had no choice but to
capitulate to Peter, whereupon she was banished to a convent.

Natalya replaced Sofia as regent. And while Ivan was maintained as co-tsar, Natalya and her advisers ran the government
for her son. Peter's new wife, a woman of scant education, shared
few of his enthusiasms, and he ignored her, except to dutifully
produce a son, Alexei.

Seemingly more important to Peter was the birth of the
Russian navy. In 1692 at Voronezh, in the southwest of the country, Peter ordered the building of a small fleet of warships. Sometimes wielding the ax or hammer himself, he used the skills he
had learned earlier from the craftsmen of the German suburb.

Two years later, Natalya died, and 21-year-old Peter at last
assumed power. In 1695-1696 the young tsar directed a successful campaign to win from the Turks the colony of Azov on

the Don River, which provided access to the Black Sea to the south. Peter would eventually make peace with the Turks, but for 21 years he would keep Russia engaged in the so-called Great Northern War, a struggle to secure an outlet to the Baltic Sea by wresting its eastern shores from Swedish domination.

Peter's hatred and mistrust of the Moscow Streltsy led him to assign their regiments to distant regions. While Peter was traveling in Europe on the great embassy, four Streltsy regiments stationed along the Polish border grew restive when, after long duty, they still awaited payment of salary in arrears and permission to return home to their families in Moscow. Disgruntled, they sent an envoy to petition Peter, and were astonished when, in the summer of 1698, they learned that the tsar had been in Europe for more than a year, having left a group of nobles in charge of the government. Resentment of their situation coupled with rumors of misgoverning led these units to march on Moscow to attempt a coup.

Peter was in Vienna when he received word of the insurrection. Furious, he exclaimed, "The seed of the Miloslavskys has sprouted again." Immediately he left the city on horseback, riding night and day with a few close associ-

MOSCOW'S KREMLIN

There is nothing above Moscow except the Kremlin, and nothing above the Kremlin except Heaven." So proclaims an old Russian proverb of the imposing kremlin, or citadel, that united Russia's secular and spiritual heritage, and which housed the seats of both the nation's government and the Russian Orthodox Church from the 14th through the 17th centuries. But Moscow's Kremlin was not Russia's first; older cities such as Novgorod, Suzdal, and Pskov already boasted proud fortifications by 1156, the year Prince Yury Dolgoruky founded a tiny hamlet on a bend of the Moscow River and enclosed it with a pine palisade to protect its inhabitants from attack. It would, though, become Russia's greatest.

The attacks on Moscow came, but the fledgling settlement survived and prospered, and by the mid-1300s more than 30,000 nobles, merchants, and craftsmen lived within its expanded walls. The transformation of the Kremlin into the architectural treasure-trove that survives today began 100 years afterward, however, when Ivan III united the surrounding lands, married the niece of the last emperor of Byzantium, and proclaimed

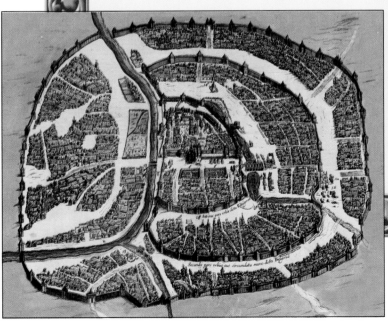

In this 17th-century map, Moscow's Kremlin nestles in the center of the city like the hub of a wheel. The Russian capital spread outward from the citadel in a series of rings, each fortified by walls and intersected by roads that led directly to the Kremlin's gates.

The Terem Palace, the residence of the tsars, contained fabulously appointed private rooms—at right, the tsarina's bedchamber, featuring an ornately carved and canopied bed and colorful tiled stove, and below, the Golden Room, a throne room and study for the tsar.

A vaulted ceiling, massive chandeliers, and murals depicting biblical and historical scenes dominate the Palace of Facets' reception hall, the Kremlin's largest throne room.

Moscow the "third Rome." He summoned the best architects and artists from Italy and Russia, commissioned a cluster of churches and palaces, and enclosed the entire complex in red stone walls studded with imposing turrets.

By the time Peter I was born in 1672, the prominence and purpose of these edifices were well established. Tsars were baptized and married in the jewel-like Cathedral of the Annunciation, crowned in the grand Cathedral of the Assumption, and buried in the silver-domed Cathedral of the Archangel Michael. In between, they lived in splendor in the Terem Palace and received nobles and visiting dignitaries in the ornate hall of the Palace of Facets.

Around the royal family, thousands of courtiers, artisans, soldiers, and ecclesiastics carried out their duties, devotions, and intrigues in the dozens of other palaces, churches, monasteries, armories, arsenals, and workshops that made up the 64-acre compound. To many, including France's last ambassador to tsarist Russia, the Kremlin, with its duality of ostentatious materialism and lofty spirituality, mirrored Russia itself, and contained within its confines "the whole epic of the Russian nation and the whole inward drama of the Russian soul."

The Cathedral of the Assumption features a five-tiered iconostasis, or icon-bearing partition, separating the altar from the nave. From 1547 on, every Russian tsar was crowned there.

ates. By the time he reached Poland, he learned that two of his army commanders had broken the rebellion, killed 130 of the Streltsy, and imprisoned nearly 2,000 more.

Upon his return to Moscow, Peter showed that he was not finished with the Streltsy. Terrifying memories of the slaughter he had witnessed as a child no doubt drove him to exact a vengeance on the jailed rebels that many considered extreme. He himself took an ax and sliced the heads from some of the insurgents. Others he subjected to horrendous tortures, scourging them with knotted whips, scorching them with flames, or breaking them on the wheel. Wrongly convinced that Sofia was behind the plot, Peter then interrogated his half sister. But she denied all involvement with the rebels, and finally Peter gave up trying to make her change her story. Instead, he forced Sofia to become a nun in the convent where she was residing, and there she remained for the rest of her life.

In the months and years ahead, Peter would turn away from bloodshed to more promising matters of state policy. He had come back from Europe with a new vision for Russia, and he was determined to harness the energies of his people to the needs of the nation, even if it required drastic reform of cherished traditions. He was disturbed, for example, by the Russian calendar, which started the year on September 1 and began, not with the birth of Christ, but with a year believed to be that of the Creation. So in Russia, the year celebrated in Europe as the turn of the century was not 1700 but 7208. Peter issued an edict bringing the calendar in line with that of western Europe.

Peter had also come back from Europe with a new, clean-shaven look and was dismayed by the appearance of the nobles of his court. He surveyed with distaste the long, fluffy beards in which Russian men delighted as symbols of manhood and dedication to the church. To the beardless monarch, this facial hair seemed merely a sign of their lack of western cultural niceties. Calling for a pair of scissors he had acquired in Holland, Peter personally cut off the flowing beards of the stunned noblemen. He then decreed that, except for clergy and peasants, all men must shave. And to enforce his edict, he refused to see any man who sought his favor unless he was beardless. After church officials objected, he modified the ruling: A man could buy a license to wear a beard; he would be issued a special bronze medallion, and while wearing it, he could do business as usual.

While abroad in the guise of a carpenter, Peter had often donned western dress. He could see its advantages over the long, loose, wide-sleeved caftans worn by Russian noblemen. These luxurious garments were richly woven of satin and brocade with high velvet collars and buttons of semiprecious stones. To face the Russian winter, a man would toss a fur cape over his caftan and don a high fur hat. In contrast to this restrictive garb, the short jackets and knee breeches worn in the West seemed to facilitate movement. Peter decreed therefore that "Hungarian or German dress" must be worn by all Russian men and women, the rich immediately, the poor within five years so that they might first wear out their old clothes. Those who appeared in public in their former finery not only would be fined but also might have their garments slashed by an inspector.

Although Russian ladies dutifully squeezed into corsets and piled on layers of skirts over a wire frame, the tsarina, alas, never had time to experiment with these new European fashions. Three days after his re-

An Old Believer—a devotee of Russian Orthodoxy and traditional Russian custom—protests as a barber dressed in European clothing prepares to lop off his beard in this 18th-century woodcut. On Peter's orders, many Russian men shaved their faces, yet saved their shorn beards so that later they could be buried with them.

turn from Europe, Peter sent Eudoxia off to a convent to become a nun, thereby securing for himself an easy divorce; his eight-year-old son, Alexei, would be raised by one of Peter's sisters. Soon after, the tsar met Martha Skavronskaya, a young Lithuanian woman who doubled as both servant and mistress to Alexander Menshikov, his closest adviser. While visiting Menshikov in 1702, Peter noticed the plump, buxom, lively Martha waiting tables, and, in the words of one of the tsar's aides, he "ended his badinage with her by saying that when he went to bed she must bring the torch to his room."

Martha became Peter's foremost mistress and trusted companion. She could restore his good humor when he fell into a rage, and even lure him out of a drunken orgy by insisting, "It's time to come home, little father." Ultimately she bore him six daughters, of whom three survived, and six sons, all of whom died as children. Peter formally married Martha—or Catherine, as she was known after her conversion to Russian Orthodoxy—in 1712, shocking the court and challenging the church, for Eudoxia was still alive. Twelve years later he formally crowned his fat, cheerful, beloved Catherine.

Soaring above his fellows from his near seven-foot height, Peter was a man of seemingly superhuman energy. He rose before dawn, and in a shabby old coat, his pockets crammed with official papers, his shoes nearly worn out, and his stockings darned, he would be at work an hour later. Although considered the richest monarch in the world, he was frugal, with little taste for luxury, and he often shocked observers with the modesty of his dress and surroundings.

Yet there were other, more troubling aspects of Peter's per-

"The money has been paid," declares the inscription on this medallion stamped with a beard and mustache, indicating that its wearer had paid a tax in order to keep his beard. Such revenues helped Peter finance his wars as well as his reforms.

sonality that kept even his most loyal associates from drawing close to him. Willful and unrestrained, he had little sensitivity for the feelings or limitations of others. When angry he could explode into verbal and even physical abuse of his companions. One courtier described Peter striking an adviser with such force that blood "spouted abundantly from the wound." On another occasion, Peter forced an elderly nobleman to sit naked for an hour on an ice floe in the Neva River, wearing only a horned hat, because the man had declined to wear a devil's costume in a masquerade. The old man then went home, took to his bed, and died.

Even when he was in more jovial moods, Peter showed a similar lack of consideration for those around him. His celebrations were marked by rowdy excesses, even during state dinners, where he brought together merchants, craftsmen, princesses, officers, diplomats, and their wives. While Peter's meals at home with his family were simple events consisting of plain dishes, as many as 300 men and women assembled at his large dinner parties to sit at tables 30 to 40 feet long. None had assigned seats, and one observer wrote of the "scuffling and fighting for chairs." At Peter's table, carpenters and shipwrights often sat by him, treating him familiarly and calling him Skipper Peter, which seemed to delight him. As soon as they were seated, the guests were required to drink a cup of brandy, followed by an assortment of other liquors. According to a visiting English merchant, on one occasion the guests got so drunk that they began to slop their drinks, dance, and even fight—and the tsar joined in.

Peter's inclination to crude practical jokes could make a dinner party an unforgettable horror for his guests. Some 70 to 80 dishes were served, but those who frequented his dinners preferred to eat at home first, for as one guest reported, Peter's cooks would "tie eight or ten young mice on a string and hide them under green peas" or submerge them in soups. When the nature of the dish was revealed, novice partygoers vomited "in a most beastly manner." For variation, "they often bake cats, wolves, ravens and the like in their pastries, and when the company have eat them up, they tell them what stuff they have in their guts."

But Peter never allowed his odd entertainments to distract him from the serious work of moving his country forward. As the Great Northern War with Sweden intensified, he began to introduce reforms that had sweeping effects on the lives of Russian citizens of every class. To fight his battles, he had to have a large, well-equipped standing army. To this end, Peter instituted a system of obligatory service for all classes. Then, as an incentive to do well in the army, he opened the ranks of the nobility to men of any origin: Those who became officers automatically became nobles. In 1705 he began to recruit many of his humblest citizens through a system of general levies that replaced the more random conscription practices of the past. Servants, craftsmen, clerks, and even serfs—peasant laborers bound by tradition and law to their masters—were drawn into the army.

Merit rather than pedigree would dictate a man's advancement in the new Russian state. Accordingly, Peter set up a Table of Ranks that linked social status to civil or military service. All Russian men, from aristocrats to commoners, would have to start at the bottom of the table, the 14th rank, and those who worked their way up to the eighth rank gained noble status.

The burgeoning army had to be financed, but the current tax system was severely flawed. The great landowners, who provided the revenue, had found ways of cheating the tax collector.

A WINDOW ON THE WEST

In a further effort to break with Russia's past, Peter decided in 1703 to abandon Moscow as the seat of his government and build a new capital for a new, westward-looking Russia. Named not for the tsar but for the apostle, St. Petersburg—seen here in a mid-18th-century view—was built by thousands of conscript workers on the swampy delta of the Neva River. Its access to the Baltic Sea would make it Russia's "window on the West."

Peter personally approved every detail of the city's construction, from the street plan to the design of houses intended for different classes of residents, as shown at right. "This great shadow of Tsar Peter pursues you ceaselessly in Petersburg," wrote a 19th-century French visitor. "It perches on all the monuments and wanders along all the embankments and through all the squares."

ORDINARY TAXPAYER'S HOUSE

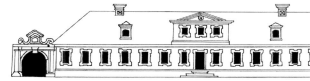

WELL-TO-DO PERSON'S HOUSE

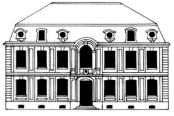

GRANDEE'S MANSION

29

To get around the tax on households, for instance, they simply decreased the number of dwellings on their properties, crowding many families into fewer wooden shacks. To evade the plow tax, they cultivated less acreage. Peter replaced these taxes with a new one. After taking a census, he imposed on landlords a tax on each individual working on their estates. This poll tax had several far-reaching consequences. First, it reduced all servants, peasants, and serfs working for a single landlord to a similar status, that of a serf bound to the land. And second, by eliminating the plow tax, more plows were used, more land was tilled, and Russian agricultural output soared.

Many of Peter's innovations met with resistance. Such was the case with educational reform, which Peter saw as a way of producing the kinds of professionals that would transform Russia. He established scores of schools throughout the country. The new schools soon lacked students, however. Bored young nobles did not want to be confined to the schoolroom, and their parents were not about to have their children whipped by schoolmasters of a lower class.

Peter was similarly rebuffed when he attempted to force the gentry to pass their estates on to their eldest sons. He wanted to keep the large estates intact; breaking them up, he believed, would lead to the ruin of both nobles and serfs. But in Russia land had traditionally been divided among all the children, including females, and the landowners resented any restriction of their right to continue that practice.

Peter's foreign ways continually clashed with the traditional Russian distrust of outsiders, and he was called an antichrist by his opponents, among whom were churchmen scandalized by his seeming lack of faith. While a Christian by conviction, Peter opposed those elements of religion that seemed to stray from the basic tenets of the faith. He opposed, for example, the practice of praying to saints.

The dissatisfaction of many nobles with Peter's policies found a champion in Peter's own son, Alexei, offspring of his former wife, Eudoxia. Unlike his father, Alexei was indolent and withdrawn, interested more in theology than technology. Peter feared Alexei would reverse his reforms when he came to power. In 1718 the tsar had his agents interrogate Alexei's mistress. The young woman gave damaging testimony against Alexei, and the 27-year-old tsarevich was soon tried for treason. He was condemned to death by a court and died in prison after severe torture and flogging.

Six and a half years later, the tsar himself died. His death was brought about by the weakening of his body after he had plunged into the frozen Neva to assist in rescuing a band of soldiers whose boat had capsized. After Peter, Russia was governed by a succession of weak rulers. By 1741 the throne had passed to Elizabeth, one of Peter's daughters from his marriage to Catherine. Unmarried and childless, Elizabeth had chosen as her successor her 14-year-old nephew, Peter, the son of a Prussian duke. And when the young man was barely 16, she scanned the princesses of Europe to find him a wife.

In January 1744, two carriages crossed the Baltic plains. The one behind carried a crew of servants; in the foremost coach rode their mistresses, Princess Sophia Augusta Fredericka and her mother, Princess Johanna Elizabeth, of the tiny Prussian principality of Anhalt-Zerbst. Their mission was secret, and at the inns along the way, they gave false names. Only when the travelers crossed the Western Dvina River and entered Russia did they reveal themselves as the invited guests of Elizabeth, empress of Russia. At the border, emissaries from the empress presented the German princesses with exquisite sable coats, while a regiment marched in their honor to the music of a brass band. "I can hardly believe that all this is for my poor self, who in her whole life has never had more than a drum beaten in her honor," Johanna wrote to her husband. It was not for Johanna, however, that the band was playing, but for her attractive 14-year-old daughter, Sophia, who was a candidate to marry the man destined to be Russia's next tsar.

Because their journey now would be through deep snow, mother and daughter traded their carriage for a Russian sleigh, a cozy little box on runners, with windows on either side. The floor was lined with silk cushions and bedding, and when the two princesses climbed in, heated stones were placed at their feet. A wax-candle lantern, suspended from the roof, rocked with the sleigh's motion as they set off. Drawn by 10 horses, the elegant sleigh was escorted by a squadron of cavalry.

About a week later, the caravan reached Moscow, where Empress Elizabeth and her court were residing for the winter. Entering the dark city at 7:00 p.m., they stopped before a brightly lighted wooden building, the Annenhof Palace. The entire court awaited them in a large hall graced with elegant crystal chandeliers. There they met Peter.

Sophia was pleased by what she saw, finding the fair-haired, narrow-shouldered 16-year-old to be friendly and "quite good-looking." Afterward, the young woman and her mother were led to a reception hall outside of the empress's bedchamber. As they had been previously instructed, the newcomers kissed Elizabeth's hand, while the empress warmly embraced both moth-

er and daughter. Sophia would later comment about Elizabeth, "It was quite impossible on seeing her for the first time not to be struck by her beauty and the majesty of her bearing."

As Sophia and her mother settled in, they were overwhelmed by the expenditures required by court life. Elizabeth and her courtiers changed their gowns three or four times a day for meals and parties. Sophia did, however, enjoy the frequent evening balls to which hundreds of people were invited. A favorite activity of the empress was to host masquerades at which men dressed as women and women as men. At one, Sophia, wearing tight hose and knee breeches, danced with a tall man struggling to move around in a wide hoop skirt. "As he gave me his hand in turning," Sophia recalled, he knocked over a countess who, in falling, sent Sophia tumbling, taking the hoop-skirted man with her. "None of us could rise without making the other two fall and eventually we had to be lifted to our feet."

Sophia was well aware that she was on trial, and from the outset, she made every effort to win over the empress. Since she spoke no Russian, she immediately started to study the language. Soon she was writing to Elizabeth in Russian, without disclosing that her letters had been written first in French, then translated by her teacher. Realizing that the devout empress would require her conversion, the Lutheran Sophia also began taking instruction in the Russian Orthodox Church. Even in sickness, she was focused on her goal: When Sophia was ill with pneumonia, her mother suggested that they call a pastor, but Sophia instead demanded the presence of an Orthodox priest. This delighted the empress, who lovingly cradled Sophia's head while a surgeon opened a vein in her foot to let out two ounces of blood.

Sophia's efforts paid off, and soon the empress arranged for the young woman's conversion ceremony and her betrothal to Peter. Standing in the chapel of the Annenhof Palace in Moscow amidst the gold, silver, and jeweled icons, Sophia read the con-

fession of faith in almost perfect Russian. With her entry into the Orthodox Church, Sophia also received a new name: Catherine. In five months, Sophia had gone far in pleasing her adoptive people.

The following summer, Catherine's marriage to Peter took place in St. Petersburg. The wedding was a lavish affair for which she wore a silver silk brocade dress, embroidered with silver flowers, snugly circling her 17-inch waist. She spent the morning arguing with Elizabeth over her hairdo. "She must wear it smooth," the empress at first declared to her hairdresser, "otherwise her jewels will not stay in place." But Catherine wanted curls, and in the end, she won; it was one of the few times she had contested Elizabeth's will.

The nobility rode to the church in a procession of 120 coaches, interspersed with brigades of Horse Guards and various marching regiments. Eight horses, a groom atop each, pulled Elizabeth's carriage, in which Catherine and Peter rode. The service was followed by dinner and a ball, from which Elizabeth sent the newlyweds home early. Catherine's ladies-in-waiting prepared her for bed, where she anxiously awaited her husband. Two hours later, Peter appeared. Giggling at the notion of finding her in bed beside him, he rolled over and promptly went to sleep.

The wedding over, there seemed little need for Johanna, and Elizabeth sent her home, thereby severing Catherine's last connection to her old life. But her new life with her husband left Catherine puzzled and uncertain. She was bewildered by Peter's immature behavior, which included

An avid rider, Catherine the Great is depicted in this equestrian portrait astride her trusted steed, Brilliant. The empress is wearing the uniform of the elite Preobrazhensky Guard.

a penchant for childish games, like blindman's buff, and more sinister occupations, such as eavesdropping on the empress and beating his dogs. He was obsessed with military exercises and playing with toy soldiers, often covering the large bed that the couple shared with miniature troops of wax and tin. Once Catherine entered the room to find a large rat, hanging from what appeared to be a noose. Peter informed her that the rat had been court-martialed and found guilty of a capital crime, eating two of his toy soldiers.

Peter continued to show no interest in consummating their marriage, and Elizabeth's impatience with the young couple grew. She blamed Catherine for not being more attentive to Peter, appointed

After seven years of marriage, as pressure to produce an heir reached a fever pitch, Catherine decided to take a lover, perhaps with Elizabeth's encouragement. Although she had been attracted to several men over the years, she had remained faithful to her husband. Now Sergei Saltykov, a handsome courtier, became her lover. Following two miscarriages, in 1754 Catherine at last gave birth to a son, Paul.

As soon as the baby arrived, he was borne away by the empress, who doted upon him. When a noblewoman suggested that he did not look like his father, Elizabeth became furious. If he is a bastard, she retorted, "he is not the first that has been in my family." Left unattended on her hard delivery bed adjoining the em-

> ## "It was quite impossible on seeing her for the first time not to be struck by her beauty."

courtiers to spy on the newlyweds, and virtually locked them together in their bedroom at night. Any person with whom they formed a close friendship was soon removed from their company.

Isolated with a man who showed no interest in her, Catherine grew despondent and threw herself into a variety of activities. She began a serious, lifelong study of the classical works of history and philosophy. But she loved the outdoor life, too, spending hours galloping through the countryside, starting out with the prim sidesaddle expected of women but then riding fully astride her horse as soon as she was out of sight. And when staying at Oranienbaum, a country palace on the Gulf of Finland, often she would rise at 3:00 a.m. to dress in a man's clothes and shoot ducks in the nearby canals.

press's chambers, the exhausted Catherine begged to be taken to her own comfortable quarters. But those nursing her were afraid of moving her without the consent of the midwife. And on the orders of the empress, the midwife was not allowed to leave the newborn. Outside her window, Catherine could hear the church bells ringing and the sounds of people dancing and singing in the streets. "Nobody worried about me," she recalled. "Half dead with fatigue and thirst, at last I was carried into my bed and did not see a soul again for the rest of the day nor did anyone come to ask after me."

While her son's birth was celebrated throughout the nation, the festivities largely excluded Catherine, who was confined to bed for 40 days and remained ill and weak for the rest of the year.

She rarely saw her baby, and wrote that she "had news of him only furtively, for to ask for news would have seemed to express doubt about the care the empress was giving him." To compound her loneliness, her lover, Saltykov, was sent abroad.

With the birth of an heir, Catherine and Peter enjoyed greater freedom. Peter turned away from her and "was almost always ill-tempered with me," Catherine complained. He openly took a mistress, Elizabeth Vorontsov, a vapid, rather plain-looking woman who belonged to one of Russia's prominent families. In the course of the next six years, Catherine herself would take two more lovers. The second of these was an officer in the guards, Grigory Orlov—more than six feet tall, muscular, handsome, daring, and some five years her junior. Legend has it that Catherine saw him one day from her window and immediately fell in love. Soon afterward she became his mistress.

Catherine was six months pregnant with Orlov's child when Elizabeth died on December 25, 1761, and Peter was proclaimed Emperor Peter III. During the traditional six-week mourning period, Catherine dressed in black, her pregnancy concealed beneath stiff crinoline underskirts, and she took care to spend hours each day on her knees by the side of Elizabeth's body as it lay in state. When the country's grieving citizens passed the open coffin, they were pleased by this show of devotion and piety. Her behavior contrasted with Peter's occasional visits to the empress's bier, during which he flirted with the ladies-in-waiting and laughed at the priests.

Peter was unpopular from the earliest days of his reign. At that time, Russia was on the verge of victory in a war against Frederick II of Prussia. Yet Peter, who had remained attached to his native Prussia, idolized Frederick. Rather than dictate the terms of the enemy surrender, as he was in a position to do, Peter allowed Frederick to keep his original territories. As if this were not insult enough to his own fighting men, Peter also changed the Russian army uniforms to look like those of the Prussians.

Having thereby alienated the military, Peter went on to cut himself off from the powerful Orthodox Church. He had been raised Lutheran, and though his conversion

Like his wife, Catherine, Emperor Peter III was of German descent, and as two foreigners in an unfamiliar environment, they had, in the beginning, become friends. But the more Russian Catherine became, the more Peter, who clung to his Prussian heritage, distanced himself from his wife.

to Orthodoxy had been required, he had never taken to his new religion. Now Peter confiscated all church property and ordered the priests to shave their beards and dress like German Protestant pastors.

A few months after Elizabeth's death, Catherine secretly gave birth to Grigory Orlov's son, Alexei. Given her estrangement from her husband, this time there was no question of passing him off as Peter's, and the baby was immediately sent to foster parents in the countryside. When Catherine regained her strength, she found that Peter's standing among the courtiers had reached a new low. Surrounded by sycophants, including his mistress Elizabeth Vorontsov, the emperor did not seem to realize how quickly he was losing popular support. Meanwhile, Catherine, wrote a French ambassador of the time, "more and more captures the hearts of the Russians."

But Catherine was in grave danger, for as she herself noted, Peter "wanted to marry Elizabeth Vorontsov and arrest me." His reported plan was to place her in a convent and disinherit her son; he went so far as to call her a

ROYAL RETREATS

Catherine II adored the pageantry of costume balls and week-long extravaganzas staged to celebrate public events. But when the empress needed time away from the formalities of court life, there were two special havens to which she would retire. During the long, dark Russian winter, she withdrew to her "hermitage," the private apartments she had added on to St. Petersburg's Winter Palace *(above)*. And in summer, her favorite retreat was the estate at Tsarskoe Selo, 50 miles northwest of the capital.

At the Hermitage, Catherine would entertain friends who shared her tastes for art, theater, opera, literature, parlor games, and intellectual discourse. Among her guests was the French ambassador, le Comte de Ségur, who wryly noted that "Hermitage" was a misnomer for a place where "one was struck by the size of the rooms and the galleries, by the splendor of the furniture, [by] the great number of old masters, and especially by a winter garden [that created]

In the art gallery she set up in the Hermitage, Catherine II displayed thousands of European masterpieces. The Hermitage, her favorite winter residence, also boasted a theater.

Catherine spent her days reading, writing, and signing decrees, memorandums, and letters—her signature, "Ekaterina," is shown above. "Since seven in the morning until . . . seven in the evening," she once remarked, "I have done nothing but write and read."

An informally attired Catherine walks one of her cherished English greyhounds at Tsarskoe Selo. "I have always loved animals," she wrote. "They have much more intelligence than they are given credit for."

an Italian spring amidst the Polar ices."

Despite the Hermitage's grandeur, Catherine insisted on informality within its bounds. Another guest, the German literary critic Friedrich Grimm, described dinner parties where "you draw for your place out of a hat and the Empress is often seated at a corner whilst [I] or another man of similar importance lords it in the middle." Grimm also recalled meeting with Catherine in her study. "There," he wrote, "one must settle into a comfortable armchair opposite the sofa of the Imperial Sovereign of all the Russians" and idle away the hours in talk "of things serious, gay, grave, frivolous."

Summers at Tsarskoe Selo—"the tsar's village"—were equally informal. An English visitor there noted that while in residence, Catherine "lays aside all state, and lives on the footing of as easy intimacy as possible" with family and invited company. More often than not, the empress could be found strolling the grounds. She reportedly walked up to 10 miles daily, tracking the distance with a hand-held pedometer.

fool in public. Catherine finally made the fateful decision to break with her husband. In the early morning hours of June 28, 1762, she hurried to the village of Kalinkina, three and a half miles outside St. Petersburg. She was met there by Grigory Orlov and a regiment of guardsmen loyal to her. "Hurrah for our little mother," some of the men began to shout as she arrived. Others, according to Catherine, "embraced me, kissed my feet, my hands, my dress, and called me their savior."

Stopping along the way to garner the loyalty of two other key regiments, Catherine rode to the capital under the protection of the soldiers. The bells soon tolled at the Kazan Cathedral after the priests inside had blessed her as "autocrat Catherine II." Next she entered the Winter Palace, where she was met by her eight-year-old son, Paul, still in his nightclothes. From the palace balcony, Catherine and Paul faced a cheering crowd in the square below.

Later that evening, Catherine donned guard's clothing—the former Russian-style uniforms, for as soon as the soldiers had received word of the coup, they had discard-

"Eager as a five-year-old," Catherine loved to play with the youngest members of her family at Tsarskoe Selo (above). "My grandchildren and great-grandchildren say that their games are never so merry as when I am there."

In a formal dining room at Tsarskoe Selo, the table is shaped like the Cyrillic letter *E* in honor of two imperial hostesses: Catherine—Ekaterina—and Empress Elizabeth.

In the famous double portrait at left, Empress Catherine stands beside a table bearing the symbols of her royal authority: the scepter, the orb, and the imperial crown. Commissioned from a Swiss jeweler for Catherine's coronation, the crown was encrusted with diamonds and precious gems from India, Brazil, Siberia, and elsewhere in Russia, and topped with a 399-carat ruby.

At her coronation ceremony on September 22, 1762 *(right)*, Catherine boldly placed the crown on her own head, as all Russian monarchs did in order to symbolize their anointing by God alone. Then, taking the scepter in her right hand and the orb in her left, she greeted those assembled to pay her homage in the Kremlin's Cathedral of the Assumption.

ed the Prussian dress mandated by Peter—and led a procession of 14,000 troops out of St. Petersburg to face her husband. But Peter mustered little resistance. Within a few hours, he was arrested and taken to Ropsha, a country estate 15 miles outside the capital, where he was imprisoned. A few days later, against Catherine's orders but perhaps not against her wishes, he was killed. The explanation given Catherine was that it was during a quarrel, but later it was whispered that Peter had been strangled by Alexei Orlov, one of Grigory's brothers, who believed this act necessary to secure the new ruler's position. Catherine released a public statement attributing Peter's death to "hemorrhoidal colic." Moving quickly to prolong the momentum of popular sentiment behind her, she began the arrangements for a grand coronation ceremony.

No longer the capital but still the symbol of Russia's old traditions and its Orthodox faith, Moscow had continued to be the site of imperial coronations. So it was that on Sunday, September 22, 1762, Catherine stood dressed in a purple robe in the Kremlin's Cathedral of the Assumption, holding a scepter and an imperial globe as she was anointed by the archbishop. The coronation was punctuated throughout the day by fireworks and cannon salutes, and at midnight the new empress walked to the Red Stairs, which led from the terrace of the Kremlin down to Red Square, to face hordes of cheering supporters who had flooded into Moscow for the occasion.

A week of public festivities followed, during which Catherine and Grigory Orlov were seen together frequently. Wherever they went, crowds cheered their appearance. Such enthusiasm was no doubt increased by the fact that Catherine had brought to Moscow 120 oak barrels crammed with silver coins, from which she had distributed to the crowds some 600,000 rubles.

At 33, Catherine was the sole ruler of a vast empire, stretching from the Polish border in the west to the Pacific Ocean in the east. Following her coronation, she plunged into her duties, setting a rigorous work schedule that she would maintain throughout her reign. Around seven in the morning she would light a fire, down a cup of black coffee, pick up a pen and paper, and set to work. Catherine scrutinized every aspect of the nation, from its educational system to its foreign affairs and its finances, usually putting in 10 to 15 hours of work a day during a six-day week. At 2:00 p.m. she broke off from her labors, and with some guests lunched on caviar, oysters, fish, duck or other game birds, or hare. Salt pork mixed with pickled cabbage was a favorite dish from her childhood; fruit was

In this 1791 English cartoon satirizing Catherine's imperial ambition and sexual appetite, the empress steps over the heads of European monarchs who, peeking under her skirts, trade lascivious remarks. A French version of the cartoon showed her bare breasted.

served, and sour cream accompanied most dishes. With her meal Catherine usually drank a glass of wine or fruit juice, diluted with water.

The impression Catherine made in person has been described as "dazzling." A contemporary noted her "broad and open" forehead, "sweetly fresh" mouth, "somewhat plump" chin, "chestnut-colored" hair, dark brown eyebrows, hazel eyes that glowed in the light with "a bluish tint," and an "almost aquiline" nose. It was a time when most Russian women, even peasants, made generous use of cosmetics. They lavished a thick coat of white paint over face, neck, and arms, achieving a doll-like appearance with a splash of red on each cheek. But Catherine seldom wore cosmetics, appearing pale, yet naturally appealing.

The empress seemed to embody the personal qualities that characterized the Enlightenment, during which she reigned. It was her iron will, high intelligence, courage, and self-control that had enabled her to achieve her ambitions. Propelled in all her tasks by an enormous energy, she was able to carry them out through a combination of optimism, open-mindedness, and pragmatism as well as her ability as a natural leader. She was gracious and pleasant, with an excellent sense of humor, and she made those who barely knew her feel like longtime friends, while those close to her adored her and were intensely loyal. Emanating charm, she had an ability to inspire respect and affection that was labeled by a contemporary as "astonishing magic." In dealing with her officials her technique was to "praise in a loud voice and scold in a whisper." But such a scold could sting, as one functionary discovered when arriving late for work. After listening to Her Majesty's praise for his father's punctuality, he turned away in shame.

Soon after Catherine's coronation, Grigory Orlov pressed her to marry him. She managed to hold him off indefinitely, while remaining his mistress. After nearly a dozen years of chafing in his undefined role, Grigory grew restless and had a series of affairs. Catherine herself then took another lover and disentangled her emotions from Grigory. She did not punish Grigory for straying, but maintained his friendship and allowed him to retain his lofty governmental posts. Moved by her generous spirit, Grigory spent a large part of his fortune to buy Catherine a 199-carat diamond cut in a high rosette more than an inch thick. She had the diamond placed in the imperial scepter.

After they drifted apart, Catherine had several other lovers, selecting increasingly younger men as she got older. The man to whom she was most deeply attached was probably Grigory Potemkin, a lieutenant general about 10 years her junior. She referred to him in letters as "my dear husband," but if they were secretly married, the fact remained hidden. They had an intense two-year relationship during which he became her trusted adviser on military, diplomatic, and domestic issues, and Catherine continued to rely on Potemkin's counsel even as their romantic attachment dissipated.

Tongues continually wagged at court concerning Cather-

ine's sexual appetites. Reflecting on the issue of sexuality, Catherine once commented, "All that can be said in opposition to it will appear but a prudery quite out of harmony with the natural instinct of the human heart."

Catherine introduced a new level of splendor to the Russian capital, and while at court she liked to wear the latest fashions from France. It was a taste echoed by her courtiers. Spectacular pearls, emeralds, and other precious jewels, for example, were fixed to the headdresses, tailored French gowns, and lavish furs of women as well as to the robes, epaulets, buttons, buckles, and sword scabbards and hilts worn by men, prompting one British noblewoman to wonder who were the more lavishly dressed, the women or the men.

In addition to the great sums spent on entertainment, money also flowed freely to the arts. Catherine ordered the construction of a series of magnificent buildings, massive yet graceful palaces, several of them architectural wonders, whose styles were copied by the nobility for their own private villas. Among the most notable was her addition to the Winter Palace. Known as the Hermitage, it was her private residence within the Winter Palace and included a separate building to house most of the numerous paintings and sculptures that she commissioned or amassed. The Hermitage would become one of the world's great art museums.

In the Hermitage she built a theater, where admission was free to

Students of the Smolny Institute, the school for girls founded by Catherine in 1764, perform a dance. The empress was very proud of the achievements of the young women at Smolny. "They make astonishing progress," she wrote to her friend Voltaire. "Their conduct is justly regarded as blameless."

This document authorized the establishment of the Moscow Orphanage, where youngsters were taught not just reading and writing but also science and foreign languages. Catherine bestowed on the orphanage the double-headed eagle seal shown above, which was used as a stamp granting free postage.

courtiers, officers, and even servants, and she encouraged a lively interest in drama. She herself became a playwright, completing five plays in 1772 during her first burst of creativity, then six comedies and three historical dramas in 1786, all heavily influenced by Shakespeare's works, which she introduced into Russia. She also wrote the librettos for a number of operas.

Just as Catherine had tried to make a pleasing impression on the Russians by embracing Russian ways, now she set out to win lasting fame throughout Europe by presenting herself as an advocate of the West's most advanced ideas. She corresponded with great European philosophers, such as Voltaire and Diderot, and used her ample funds to support artists, writers, and any other intellectuals who might join the chorus of those applauding her. She encouraged the publication of books and periodicals by licensing private publishing houses. As a result, journalism flourished, and many works of western literature were translated into Russian, a spur to Russian writers. The independence of some of these authors, however, eventually led her to introduce a system of censorship to be enforced by local police chiefs. When Diderot visited her in St. Petersburg and criticized her method of governing, she had a ready answer: A philosopher's thoughts were in the clouds, while she had to "write laws on human skin."

Devoted to education, Catherine was determined to create model citizens molded by boarding schools. She encouraged such schools for girls as well as boys and, in 1782, set up a commission to develop a system that would spread learning beyond the rich few. A teacher's college was established, and eventually the government opened schools in a number of towns until, by the end of the 18th century, there were 3,154 schools teaching about 20,000 students, some 2,000 of them girls.

Having found commissions an effective means of bypassing the regular government, Catherine in 1767 called together a commission of 565 representatives to restructure the laws. One individual was sent from each of 208 towns; 161 came from the nobility, 28 were government appointees drawn from the bureaucracy, 79 were elected by peasants on government-owned estates, and the rest represented Cossacks and other national minorities. In preparation, Catherine drew up a remarkable document known as the Nakaz, or Instruction. Crammed with progressive legal principles derived from the most forward-looking western European philosophy, the empress's treatise was praised throughout the intellectual world. But much of the material was struck from the document in advance of the commission hearings by Russian churchmen and nobles, whom she first consulted. The remaining articles were ratified by the commission, then locked up in the royal archives and thereafter ignored.

Catherine had opened the door to discussions of reform, but her frequent professions of liberalism bore little fruit. In fact, she even

At heart an autocrat, Catherine was horrified as she absorbed news of the French Revolution and determined to take harsh measures against any opposition to her rule. When idealistic nobleman Alexander Radishchev wrote a treatise critical of her regime entitled *Journey from St. Petersburg to Moscow,* she was appalled. In the guise of a series of travel sketches, Radishchev exposed the terrible suffering of peasants and serfs.

Catherine gave the book a thorough reading, making stinging comments in the margins, then ordered the arrest of "the rebel." Radishchev's trial aroused enormous interest in the book, now banned. Despite house-to-house searches for the publication, volumes were secreted, and some were copied by hand and passed around or sold for as much as 100 rubles. Radishchev was condemned to death, a verdict that offered Catherine an opportunity to

"Too much laughing had given her slight symptoms of colic."

revoked one of the few rights still left to the serfs, that of petitioning the Crown for redress against harsh treatment by a landowner, a right encouraged by Peter the Great and often exercised during his reign. By her decree, those making such a complaint could be flogged and forced to labor in Siberian exile.

Little wonder that her era was considered a golden age of the nobility; for the serfs, however, conditions worsened. In her waning years, the empress faced mounting complaints as the economy declined, drained by the extravagant splendor of her court and the costs of maintaining an army constantly at war. It was a highly successful army, however, for its victories in the Crimea and Poland gave Russia control of those lands, affording the country its long-dreamed-of access to the Black and Baltic Seas.

exhibit her mercy; she commuted the sentence to exile in Siberia, and he was promptly dispatched to the frozen wasteland in an open carriage, heavily guarded and in chains.

Six years later, in 1796, the empress's health was fast waning. She was described by one observer as having "increased in size, so as to be an object almost of deformity." Yet resplendent in her diamonds, she still basked in the veneration of the diplomats and courtiers who packed her throne room. One evening she retired earlier than usual, explaining that "too much laughing had given her slight symptoms of colic." The next day she suffered a stroke and soon afterward, she died. The 35-year reign of Catherine the Great had opened Russia further to the political and social currents that would surge through Europe in the years to come.

AT WAR WITH NAPOLEON

Thrust into power in 1801 by the assassination of his father, Paul, Tsar Alexander I hoped to restore the enlightened rule of his grandmother, Catherine II. Instead he found himself at war with Napoleon Bonaparte, emperor of France. After several defeats, Alexander sued for peace.

In 1807 the two leaders met at Tilsit, on the Prussian-Russian border. Arriving on either side of the Neman River, they met, in a gesture of parity, on a tented raft moored midway, pictured here in the idealized empire style. Stepping aboard the raft, the emperors embraced, the diminu-

tive Corsican's head barely reaching above the chest of the strapping Alexander. They exchanged embroidered handkerchiefs and repartee.

Although Alexander salvaged some of his country's dignity, he also made tremendous concessions. He grievously betrayed his Prussian allies and agreed to join France in her boycott of British goods. Napoleon wrote afterward of the accord, cynically alluding to "the fine phrases I dropped at Tilsit." As Alexander was to learn, the treaty did not buy peace, only time.

The forces of Field Marshal Barclay de Tolly *(far right)* gave their all at the walled city of Smolensk *(below)*, but Bagration *(right)* made no effort to aid them. His disdain for Barclay led him to cry on the eve of battle, "For God's sake, send me anywhere, if only to command a regiment in Moldavia."

THE BATTLE OF SMOLENSK

Outraged by the treaty signed at Tilsit, many Russians decried the tsar's alliance with "the antichrist," as the Orthodox Church called Napoleon, and resented the boycott on British goods. As relations between Russia and France steadily deteriorated, no one questioned that war would come again.

And so it did. On June 24, 1812, Napoleon's troops, some 400,000 strong, thundered across the Neman. Not since the eighth-century invasion by Arabs and Berbers had Europe seen such a force. Napoleon hoped for a quick, decisive engagement, but while Alexander raised rubles and conscripts, his outmanned troops eluded the French. In search of a battle, Bonaparte allowed himself to be drawn into the Russian interior.

Reaching Smolensk on August 16, Napoleon saw his chance to fight. Two of the tsar's largest armies had halted near the sacred walled city of Smolensk. One of them, led by Field Marshal Mikhail Barclay de Tolly, occupied the city and was prepared to defend it.

To the east was the army of General Pyotr Bagration, whose antipathy for the field marshal kept him from ordering his troops to come to the defense of either the city or Barclay's men.

The French mounted a two-day-long assault on Smolensk. The Russians fought with awesome ferocity; the wounded stood their ground until they dropped, and civilians perished in the cross fire. After nightfall, rather than risk annihilation, Barclay ordered a retreat. Cossacks rode through the ruins igniting powder stores, setting the city ablaze. When Napoleon awoke on the 18th, he found he had been deprived once again of his decisive battle.

As an officer waits to take him away, a conscripted serf's father offers a blessing and his mother is consumed with grief.

THE BATTLE OF BORODINO

Mikhail Kutuzov, the 67-year-old commander who replaced Barclay, was a crafty and unpredictable tactician. Although Borodino (below) technically was won by the French, Kutuzov's skill denied Napoleon the decisive victory he so eagerly sought.

After the retreat at Smolensk, the conflict between Barclay and Bagration forced Alexander to appoint another commander in chief, Prince Mikhail Kutuzov. Kutuzov was an experienced veteran, though not a favorite of the tsar. His left eye had been shot out, and his corpulent belly frequently prevented him from mounting a horse. Nevertheless, he was beloved by both the army and the people, and was as cunning as ever. With his army still outmanned by the French, Kutuzov led them further into Russia.

Napoleon's army, doggedly seeking engagement, followed. Violent rainstorms turned the roads to boot-sucking mud, stranding their wagons. Scorching heat then baked the muddy ruts to stone, tripping men and horses and breaking their legs. The route was illuminated by fires in the fields, deliberately set to deprive the enemy of provision. One foot soldier remembered "the very great heat, the dust which was like a thick fog, the closed line of columns, and the putrid water from the holes filled with dead people, and cattle." Two weeks and 200 miles later, on September 6, 1812, they reached Borodino. Kutuzov was already there.

The next day, the surrounding hills bristled and boomed with artillery, pounding both sides. The armies fought savagely, and the toll was ferocious. Bagration, his leg shattered, was killed. Armand de Caulaincourt, foreign minister to Napoleon, reported that "almost every division and several of the regiments had lost their commanding officers, killed or wounded."

It was as if neither side could manage to get a grasp on victory. Napoleon stood sullen at a high vantage point, undistracted as cannonballs screamed and thudded to the ground around him. "These Russians let themselves be killed as if they were not men, but mere machines," he marveled.

The slaughter was beyond imagining. The French, with their supply lines stretched to the breaking point, were desperately underequipped to treat their casualties. Untrained soldiers assisted the surgeons at candlelit amputations. Thousands died from exposure, infection, and neglect.

Only night brought an end to the fighting. This time, bleeding and depleted, both sides staggered into retreat.

Hundreds of the citizens who remained in Moscow were put to death for arson. In a communiqué to Alexander, Napoleon described "streets littered with dead men . . . hanged or shot. Beside them stands a placard reading, 'Incendiaries of Moscow.' "

"Arm yourselves!" Governor General Feodor Rostopchin exhorted his citizens before he himself fled. Rostopchin is thought to have encouraged the fires that consumed most of the city *(below)*.

THE BURNING OF MOSCOW

It took six days for the remnants of the French army to stumble the 60 miles from Borodino to Moscow. Kutuzov, though urged by Alexander and his generals to fight, decided on September 13 to retreat. "Napoleon is like a stormy torrent which we are as yet unable to stop. Moscow will be the sponge that will suck him in," he assured them.

Moscow's citizens had not waited for this news. For days after Borodino, carriages and droshkies rumbled over the roads leading east as tens of thousands of Muscovites fled the city. Hordes took off on foot, pushing babies and belongings in wheelbarrows, carrying what little provision they could.

On the afternoon of September 14, Napoleon spied the golden domes of Moscow. Now it was just a short ride ahead to claim the capital and be greeted with deference by an emissary of the people.

But there was no emissary; in fact, there were no people. The troops entered the city only to the echoing sound of their own footsteps. Broad avenues, narrow alleys, sturdy homes, and ornate palaces all stood silent and empty. "Moscow," a witness wrote, "seems to us to be a huge corpse . . . the kingdom of silence."

But what a kingdom! Seduced by its Byzantine splendor and troves of abandoned luxuries, French soldiers began looting. When, toward nightfall, wisps of smoke began to rise, they were attributed to accidental fires set by disorderly troops.

Napoleon was asleep before his generals realized that they were wrong. Within hours, fire after fire swept through the city. The empty city, in fact, harbored an army of arsonists. Those caught in the act were shot on sight; others were tried and hanged. Napoleon, awakened, gazed at the brilliant night and exclaimed, "To burn down one's own cities! . . . What savage determination! What a people! What a people!"

When rains eventually put out the flames, four-fifths of the city was in ashes. While delicacies remained abundant, the army was fast running out of staples—plenty of jam but no bread. Napoleon had assumed—incorrectly—that the occupation of Moscow would cause Alexander to plead for peace. After five weeks of lingering in the ruins of his dreams, Napoleon led his men west from Moscow for the 1,500-mile trek home.

Two French grenadiers struggle to stand in a snowstorm *(right).* Thousands succumbed to the bitter cold. But it was at the Berezina River, drawn from memory by a survivor *(below),* that the army suffered its worst blow.

Seeming to come from out of nowhere, bands of Cossacks struck at French troops on the torturous retreat from Moscow. These wild tribesmen, descended from generations of southern Russian outlaws, proved a ruthless and relentless foe throughout the journey.

THE FRENCH RETREAT

Some 80,000 men began to make their way back with Napoleon. At first, in a spirit more like that of a carnival than of a campaign, horses pulled wagons piled high with booty. When icy autumn rains came, the procession slowed to a painful crawl. Occasionally bands of peasants attacked the men with pitchforks and axes, and herds of howling Cossacks plagued the troops, picking off stragglers.

After snow fell, the men gradually abandoned their plunder over the frozen roads. One soldier remembered seeing "candelabras, whole libraries, gold and silver crucifixes, chalices, beautiful carpets" lying in roadside ditches.

Filthy and in tatters, thousands died of the cold. Others, absurdly, were swathed in stolen capes, carpets, and tapestries. A French foot soldier recalled the surreal scene. "It was not possible to recognize one another except by voice. Everyone was disguised. . . . they wore round hats and peasant caps. . . . many had priests' robes from the churches. It was like a world turned upside down."

On November 26 they approached the Berezina River. The water was frigid but not frozen, and swollen from floods. As French engineers attempted to build bridges, the troops panicked. Humans and horses pressed to the shore, trampling each other. As the bridges were finished, thick snow fell. Many still riding toppled into the water as their horses lost their footing on the loose pontoons. Soon thousands of the frozen dead bobbed among the ice floes. Throughout, Cossacks fired at the miserable mass. By the end of the day, 15,000 French had been taken prisoner by the Russians, and 6,000 more were dead.

Early the next morning, on Napoleon's orders, the bridges were destroyed. Anyone on the eastern shore was left to the mercy of the Cossacks and the cold.

THE TRIUMPHANT ALLIES ENTER PARIS

The 40,000 or so troops who crossed the Neman back toward France represented less than a tenth of those who had followed Napoleon east. Although he tried to mount a new campaign, even calling up almost a million fresh men and boys, Napoleon's failure in Russia was the beginning of the end of his empire.

In the year that followed, a new alliance was formed between Russia, Prussia, Austria, and Britain. Alexander resumed command of his army, and on March 31, 1814, a day he later described as the happiest of his life, he led the Allies through Paris's Pantin Gate *(right)*.

The assembled crowds were awed by the spectacle. The tsar on his Arabian mount, Eclipse, marched with the Imperial Guard. The guard was followed, and upstaged, by the Cossacks with their exotic beards, cloaks, and pantaloons. Then tens of thousands of foreign troops marched down the Champs-Élysées. Alexander spoke to the French people, professing never to have had a quarrel with them and pledging his protection. Russian priests offered prayers of thanks in the square where Louis XVI had lost his head. Cossacks pitched their tents in the Bois de Boulogne.

Relieved of the grief of continued warfare, many of the French opened their arms to the Allies, and particularly to Alexander. He walked the streets unguarded, and attended soirees and the theater. He met with Kosciusko to discuss the issue of a free Poland, and with Lafayette to discuss freeing the serfs. He was hailed by some as the savior of Europe.

From Paris Alexander sailed to Britain, where he met with further adulation. He was welcomed at Westminster, Greenwich, the British Museum, and the Royal Exchange. When Allied troops paraded in Hyde Park, his troops—especially the ever colorful Cossacks—were heartily cheered.

Alexander's glory, however, was short lived. Some of his remarks, including his profession of divine guidance, aroused British suspicion. General Robert Wilson, former British liaison to Kutuzov and a member of Parliament, predicted that the tsar would use this victory as a steppingstone. He warned of a Russian invasion of India, the fall of Constantinople, and eventually all of Europe. He was wrong, but his words left a lasting impression—the image of a Russia bent on world domination.

REWARDING THE VICTORS

Alexander awarded Kutuzov the Order of St. George of the First Class *(near right),* one of the most coveted decorations given for valor in battle. Others who participated in the 1812 campaign received a medal bearing a Masonic symbol *(center)*—silver for the soldiers and bronze for noblemen and merchants. Priests were rewarded with a crucifix *(far right)* whose inscription identifies God as the reason for their bravery: "Not for us, not for us, but for you."

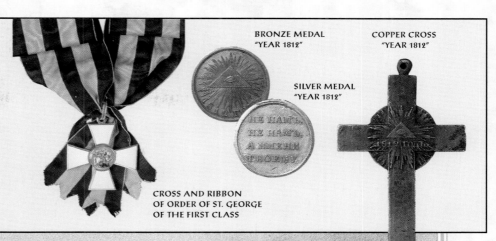

BRONZE MEDAL "YEAR 1812"

COPPER CROSS "YEAR 1812"

SILVER MEDAL "YEAR 1812"

CROSS AND RIBBON OF ORDER OF ST. GEORGE OF THE FIRST CLASS

CHAPTER TWO

LIFE ON A COUNTRY ESTATE

A dam in front of the main house at Spasskoe, a country estate not far from Moscow, symbolizes the divide between serf and master. Some grandees owned so many serfs that their properties functioned smoothly without oversight. According to one traveler, "For a Russian noble to be able to say he has never even seen his estates is something rather to boast of, for it is intended to convey the impression that his fortune is in a very flourishing condition."

From the princess Dashkova, at her estate of Troitskoe, to Mrs. Catherine Hamilton, in Dublin. April 20, 1802:

My very dear friend, how overjoyed I was to hear from you after all this time! And how happy I am to grant your request! How could you even think that I would do otherwise? Yes, I will be delighted to welcome your young cousins as my guests when they visit Russia. The Misses Wilmot must feel free to stay with me as long as they like—or as long as their loving parents can endure their absence. I flatter myself that life here at Troitskoe is not without its amenities and comforts. And I shall do everything in my power to make them happy. My only sorrow is that you yourself cannot accompany them.

Captain Wilmot and his lady are to be commended for this enlightened approach to their daughters' education. Nothing, as I'm sure you agree, broadens the mind like a sojourn beyond one's own native land.

How well I remember my own first taste of foreign travel! At the time, I was still reeling from the shock of early widowhood, fearful for my children's futures, plagued by financial worries, and out of favor at court. Yet once I received Empress Catherine's permission to leave for foreign parts, I began to breathe again.

And what consolations awaited me—encounters with such remarkable thinkers as Monsieur Diderot, breathtaking landscapes, warm hospitality, and, most rewarding of all, the beginning of our mutual friendship! I still cherish the memories of our tour of the magnificent Scottish Highlands, our happy seasons together at Spa and Aix-en-Provence, our visit to the immortal philosopher Voltaire.

Is it really 18 years since your own visit? Laugh at me if you will, but the scarf you gave me then still rests upon my neck, although—like the flesh beneath—it is now somewhat the worse for wear. But other things are scarcely changed since those happy days. The gardens demand as much of my time as ever. (How kind you were, coming from those islands that are the founts of all horticultural wisdom, about my own efforts at landscaping and garden design!) And even now, as I sit at the writing desk in the library you loved so well, looking out at my forests, your old friend Marfa busies herself in the corner of the room, muttering her usual litany of complaints as she replenishes the wood in the stove.

Yes, spring at Troitskoe still brings chilly evenings. But only the smallest traces of snow remain, and the fruit trees are coming into blossom. And today, for the first time this year, I will have fresh flowers to grace my dining table.

But time, alas, does not stand still. Do you remember our visit to the peasants in the new village I named Hamilton in your honor? Those little girls in embroidered skirts, who entertained you with their native songs and dances, still live there—but now they have small dancing daughters of their own! And those cousins of yours, who were but children then, are now ladies preparing to travel independently abroad!

I cannot tell you how much I look forward to receiving your Miss Martha and—when the time is ripe—Catherine. Because they are kin to you, how could I do other than to cherish them as if they were my own flesh and blood? In the warm seasons I will regale the Misses Wilmot with all the delights and diversions Troitskoe affords. Then, when winter forces our migration into town, I promise the most glittering balls and entertainments that Moscow has to offer. If you fear that I shall spoil them, then I can only say, my dear, that you are right!

May God grant you good health and every blessing,
Your loving friend, Catherine Dashkova

Princess Catherine Dashkova, an intellectual leader during the reign of Catherine the Great, fell in and out of favor at court and eventually retired to the country. There she spent the last years of her life, taking a personal interest in the daily running of her estate, Troitskoe.

Martha Wilmot, a wellborn young Irish woman, remained as a guest at Troitskoe for five years, during which time she became like a daughter to Princess Dashkova. In addition to learning about Russian country life, she was presented at court and mingled with the most influential nobility of the day.

Late on a hot August afternoon in 1803, Miss Martha Wilmot arrived at Troitskoe. Sent on this trip in the hope that it would be a respite and would help assuage her grief over the death of her favorite brother, the 28-year-old felt only more anxious as she stepped from the carriage. She had broken her long journey with a stop in St. Petersburg, where she had heard some unpleasant gossip about Princess Dashkova. "She was represented to me," Martha recalled, many years later, "as a most cruel and vindictive person." The young foreigner was warned that Troitskoe itself was a bleak fortress whose sinister chatelaine would probably censor Martha's mail.

But now, striding across the lawns, brushing the dirt of a day's gardening off her hands, came an eccentric-looking dowager. The princess dressed for comfort rather than style: On this particular afternoon, she wore a man's cap and something that looked like a dressing gown. She instantly put Martha at her ease, greeting her in fluent English.

"Her appearance is milder than I expected," confided Martha in a letter home. She praised the princess's warm smile and easy manner, and spoke of "a certain something that distinguishes her not unpleasingly from the common herd." Nor was Troitskoe itself quite as grim as anticipated. Her hostess displayed a reassuringly "English taste" in domestic arrangements. "She has really created from rather a barren situation one of the most lovely and magnificent places that is to be found anywhere!"

For the next five years, Martha Wilmot would live with the Princess Dashkova, almost as a surrogate daughter of the house. Her older sister Catherine would join her in 1805, but leave without her two years later. Their minutely detailed journals and letters home to Ireland would provide an invaluable and honest record of life among the Russian aristocracy.

Troitskoe was set in acres of woodland some 50 miles southwest of Moscow. Dominated by the princess's own spacious mansion, the estate was a world of its own. In addition to the stables, staff quarters, barns, dairy, and other agricultural outbuildings that no self-respecting landowner could dispense with, the princess had also constructed hothouses for cultivating tropical fruits, a private theater, a riding academy, a heated bathhouse, and paved walks that led through lawns and shrubberies to a variety of rustic fol-

GROWING UP ON THE ESTATE

Like aristocratic children everywhere, youngsters who grew up on Russia's country estates lived in a different world from that of their parents. For Russian children, this separation began early, with a serf wet nurse taking charge of a newborn and, later, a serf nanny taking over.

Nannies, such as the older woman shown here with a wealthy couple and their three children, provided children with their first religious training and shared with them stories from the folklore of old Russia. After leaving the nursery, boys and girls were educated separately, and exposure to their Russian heritage was replaced by the adoption of the Western values and tastes of their parents.

Normally boys were taught at home by foreign-born tutors for a few years before being sent to boarding schools and then on to careers in the military or the civil service. Girls usually stayed at home, and governesses taught them the practical and social skills they would later employ as mistresses of their own estates. When these young women had children, they would seek out a devoted nanny to care for their young, and the whole process would begin again.

lies and pretty retreats. Martha, in a meditative mood, could stroll along the banks of a nearby river, daydream in a miniature Chinese temple, or meander up winding paths shaded by birch trees.

Within the house's white-stuccoed walls, Martha found magnificent reception rooms, imposing stone staircases, a warren of bedchambers, a self-contained guest wing, a library stocked with thousands of volumes, a ballroom, and a picture gallery lined with ancestral portraits. The floors and furniture were inlaid with wood of many kinds and different colors, and they were polished to a lapidary luster.

Martha's day began at 7:30 in the morning. She breakfasted on coffee in her own "most cheerful, agreeable, and well furnished apartment." A maidservant then appeared with a bowl containing a lump of ice. This, Martha learned, was for rubbing on the

Just after their repast, the ladies of the house repaired to the drawing room for a peaceful spell with their books or needlework. But, unless the weather forbade it, no day was complete without a few hours of walking in the fresh air. Then, with their appetites restored, the household reconvened for dinner.

There were plenty of breaks in this routine—picnics; excursions to neighboring mansions; swimming in the river; tours of the estate to watch the serfs at their labors in the fields and workshops; courtesy calls on elderly peasant women in smoky cottages; visits to the village church on Sundays and holy days. Sometimes, Martha reported, these rites were canceled because the priest was too drunk to lead the prayers. And if Princess Dashkova objected to a cleric's performance, she didn't hesitate to interrupt the service and scold him for his incompetence.

"Think of 200, 300, and often 400 servants to attend a small family."

cheeks to produce the rosy complexion deemed essential by every aristocratic Russian belle. After a quiet morning spent reading, practicing music, or writing letters, Martha would join the princess in her own room for an hour's conversation: "We chat, sometimes about Kings and Empresses and sometimes about Wheat and rye."

Lunch was served at 2:00 p.m. Martha approved of the Troitskoe cuisine, which was based on the estate's own excellent products—fish from the river, vegetables from the field, cream and cheese from the princess's dairy. Martha's letters home told of fresh and pickled cucumbers, caviar, fish soup, salads of all descriptions, roast meat and game, all "superb and well dress'd with Cleanliness and delicacy."

Conscientious landowners such as the princess expended considerable time and energy on the management of their estates. In his memoirs, the great writer Count Leo Tolstoy recalled the hours his father spent closeted with his bailiff, examining the account books and arguing over the fine points of rents, mortgages, repairs, moneys due from the sale of hay, and the financial woes of the miller, who had got himself hopelessly into debt.

To relieve the stresses of such encounters, the typical Russian nobleman would whistle up his hounds, grooms, and huntsmen, mount his favorite horse, and head for the hunting field in search of foxes, game birds, hares, bears, and wolves. Princess Dashkova, however, preferred a less conventional form of exercise: She liked to roll up her sleeves, tuck up her skirts, and get down to the business of mending walls, shoeing horses, building roads, husking corn, and curing the ills of her human and animal dependents. "She is," marveled Martha's sister Catherine, "a Doctor, an Apothecary, a Surgeon, a Farrier, a Carpenter, a Magistrate, a Lawyer."

Despite this willingness to get her hands dirty, Dashkova reigned as an absolute monarch in her own little kingdom. Luckily for those who served her, the princess seemed a relatively benevolent despot. But when she snapped her fingers, she had some 200 domestic servants at her beck and call. And Troitskoe, in comparison with many aristocratic households, was considered almost understaffed.

"It is really astonishing," reported Martha Wilmot, "but the number of servants is dreadful. Think of 200, 300, and often 400 servants to attend a small family. A Russian Lady scorns to use her own feet to go upstairs, and I do not Romance when I assure you that two Powdered footmen support her lily white elbows and nearly lift her from the ground, while a couple more follow with all manner of Shawls, Pelises, etc."

The typical aristocratic household included a number of hired professionals with specialized skills, such as tutors, governesses, physicians, music teachers, and dancing instructors. But the vast majority of those who answered to the master's call were serfs, members of peasant families whose lives, generation after generation, had been intimately intertwined with those of their noble landlords. Some of these would have been house serfs. Others would have been serf artisans apprenticed to learn a specialty, such as cabinetmaking, tailoring, or even architecture.

Like the crystal chandeliers and porcelain dinner services, serfs counted as material possessions. So when Dashkova presented Martha with a cornucopia of useful gifts, she thoughtfully included a small serf girl along with the silks, shawls, and sealing wax. Martha felt ambivalent: "My little Pashinka arrived this evening and the dear princess assures me she is now my own

property for ever. Poor little soul; she shall never find that word property abused by me."

For a Russian landowner it was a point of honor to keep all the peasant souls in his possession gainfully employed. Those who lived in the lord's villages earned their livelihoods working his fields. But there also were armies of house serfs whose existence needed to be justified somehow. If all the obvious jobs were taken, tasks had to be invented. So some noble households possessed valets or maids responsible for only one item of clothing, or minions whose sole vocation was lighting and refilling the master's pipe. At the bottom of the hierarchy toiled those who tended to ordinary housework: window washers, furniture polishers, laundresses, cooks.

As well as running these aristocratic pleasure domes, servants—like the crew on a modern cruise ship—often doubled as entertainers. Martha enjoyed the performances in Troitskoe's own elegant miniature theater, where "our laborers, our Cooks, our footmen . . . turn into Princes, Princesses, Shepherds and Shepherdesses" and perform "with a degree of spirit that is astonishing." When the curtain fell, these nymphs and heroes changed back into their usual livery in time to pass around the caviar at supper.

Hospitality on the great estates was quite lavish. It was not uncommon for guests from far away, such as the Misses Wilmot, to stay for years on end. And virtually every household had its share of supernumeraries and hangers-on. There was always room at the table for poor relations, neighbors down on their luck, old retainers, ancient nurses whose toddling charges had somehow, overnight, acquired paunches, beards, and grandchildren of their own.

Pious families also made room for the strange, seemingly simpleminded individuals who drifted from one estate to another, turning up as the spirit moved them to offer a blessing or a cryptic prophecy in return for food and shelter. Tolstoy recalled

MAGICAL RUSSIAN FOLK TALES

Folk tales have always been a part of Russia's oral tradition, and the storytellers who preserved this enduring aspect of its culture might find an audience anywhere, from a woodcutters' camp to the bedchamber of the reigning tsar.

In expectation of some sort of payment, storytellers recounted tales of heroes and princesses, ogres and dragons, flying carpets and magical quests; of the witch Baba Yaga, who lived in a forest hut raised off the ground on giant chicken feet; of Ivan the Fool, who with magical help won the hand of the tsar's daughter; and of the mythical firebird, inspiration for the ballet by Igor Stravinsky. The illustration at right, an 18th-century hand-colored print, depicts the *alkonost*, or bird of sorrow—a fantastic creature, half bird, half woman, whose story told of its power to protect or destroy any man that fell under the spell of its beauty and sweet songs.

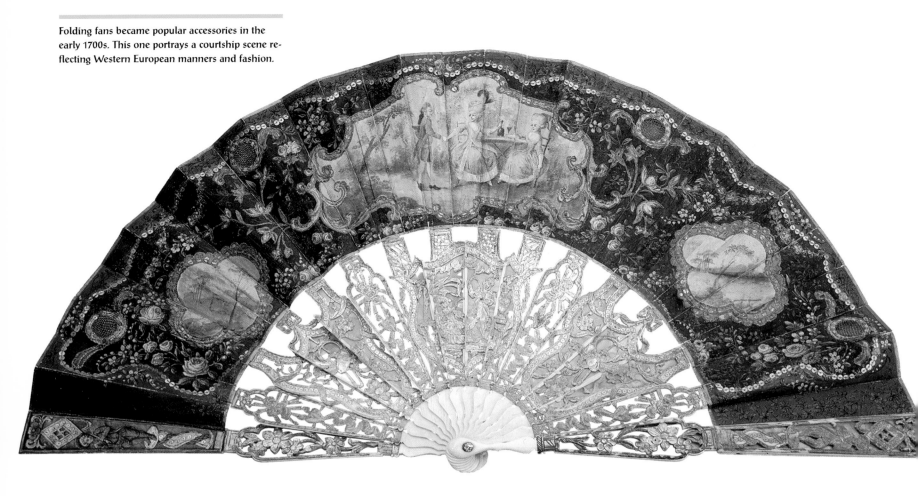

Folding fans became popular accessories in the early 1700s. This one portrays a courtship scene reflecting Western European manners and fashion.

his mother's patronage—and his father's ill-concealed dislike—of one such holy man by the name of Grisha. Barefoot whatever the weather, Grisha tended to arrive at mealtimes. He would sit at his own little table in the dining room, issuing a stream of disjointed prayers and warnings, without once lifting his eyes from his well-laden plate.

Yet even the hungry Grishas of the Russian countryside knew better than to turn up at a grandee's gates out of season. For when the blazing days of August gave way to autumnal mists and rain, the lights began to go out in the palaces. The aristocracy readied itself for its mass migration to winter quarters in Moscow or St. Petersburg.

City life held few attractions for the elderly Princess Dashko-va, who preferred to spend most of the year in her rural retreat. But during Martha's stay, there were several excursions, of varying lengths, away from Troitskoe. She took her young guest to Moscow for a taste of sophisticated society, and on an extended summertime visit to an estate she owned in Poland.

And whenever the princess traveled, she did so in style. The Polish excursion, for example, demanded a field kitchen supplied with silver dishes and wineglasses, a portable bedstead with all the necessary soft furnishings, two baggage wagons, five maids, 14 male servants, a butler, a pair of cooks, 27 horses, and three excited dogs.

The migrations of aristocrats between their urban and rural mansions demanded even more elaborate preparations, especially when the rural estate was a long trek from Moscow or St. Petersburg. In these cases, the springtime departure for the country seat was a logistical nightmare, requiring the inclusion of every article, down to the last tea leaf, that might conceivably be required for a family's comfort and delight. Baggage trains of 100 carts were not uncommon.

When the massive task of packing was complete, the entire household assembled for the traditional leave-taking ritual. Everyone sat in a circle and observed a short period of silence. Prayer was advisable, for these journeys were never undertaken lightly: The weather was capricious, the roads often hazardous, with long and lonely gaps between post stations or hospitable private houses.

To make themselves as comfortable as possible, aristocrats traveled in *kibitkas,* which reminded the Wilmots of giant cradles, large enough for four people to lie down in without crowding, or in the long, roofed surreys called *lineikas.* On winter journeys, these conveyances, fitted with sleigh runners instead of wheels, often took advantage of the iced-up rivers, gliding along them as if they were roads.

This particular option may not have been available on the route between Troitskoe and Moscow. Martha's sister, Catherine, wrote feelingly of one horrible midwinter journey over trails pockmarked with ridges and canyons of hard-packed frozen snow. "In these dreadful holes one is sometimes rooted for 20 minutes at a time, the miserable Horses falling with the exertion of pulling one out and lashed up again and again by dozens of People and servants."

But the rigors of travel brought its compensations. At journey's end lay the bright lights of Moscow. In town, Martha filled her days with interesting and self-improving pastimes—visiting the theater, paying social calls, studying Italian, taking lessons in dancing and drawing, learning how to play the guitar. At the princess's insistence, she also sat for her portrait. In fact, during

Martha's stay in Russia, Dashkova commissioned at least four different likenesses of her young friend, including two full-size oil paintings, a miniature to adorn the lid of Dashkova's own snuffbox, and another miniature to send back to Ireland as a gift for Martha's mother.

Within this packed schedule, Martha also had to find time for fittings with her dressmakers. As a temporary member of Moscow's high society, she was bombarded daily with invitations to balls, concerts, banquets, weddings, and masquerades. To hold her own among the local belles, she needed a whole new wardrobe of suitably luxurious gowns, shawls, and the jewels to go with them, for the ladies of Moscow's elite dressed to kill.

On some grand occasions, Martha found it hard to keep a straight face as she contemplated her fellow guests' ornate costumes. At one princely wedding, Martha encountered a lady who resembled "a perfect Jeweller's Shop." Her costume consisted of an embroidered white satin robe swagged with garlands of artificial flowers; two pairs of diamond headbands and diamond combs; a diamond tiara; ropes of pearl and yet more diamonds; a bosom ablaze with diamond, ruby, and emerald brooches; a diamond belt clasped with a huge crimson jewel "as large as a hen egg," set in a diamond frame.

But it wasn't only the women who went in for such lavish accessories. Peering over the brim of her champagne glass, Martha observed their spouses, sons, and even their aged fathers "tottering under the weight of Diamonds and Pearls." She was particularly struck by one Count Alexei Orlov, a great brute of a man who displayed his devotion to his empress by wearing her portrait enclosed in a frame of massive diamonds, and covered not by the usual piece of glass but by a single, smooth diamond of prodigious size.

Thus arrayed, the Moscow elite came together for such strenuous revels as four-hour banquets that featured out-of-season delicacies, grapes "as large as Pigeons' Eggs," and gargantuan trays of meat and fish that just kept on coming, 50 or 60 courses in swift succession. The sight of such excess saddened Martha: "Many a time have I wished the wasted food of their fatiguing feasts transported to little Erin, which too often wants what is here despised."

In between these orgies of consumption, the guests took to the dance floor or enjoyed elaborate theatrical and musical entertainments. Hosts vied with one another to provide the most memorable spectacles. The same Count Orlov who wore his empress's likeness set in diamonds owned a private serf orchestra of 40 horn players.

At a ball to welcome in the New Year of 1806, Martha and her new friends first watched an elaborate shadow play, consumed a magnificent supper, and admired an allegorical tableau of the dawn goddess, Aurora, in her golden chariot opening the gates of morning. Afterward they repaired to the ballroom, danced the popular polonaise, then went outdoors to watch their hosts' servants attempt—unsuccessfully—to launch a hot air balloon.

When these diversions palled, there was no shortage of witty conversation. In the salons of Moscow and St. Petersburg, the discourse was almost always conducted in French, by a westward-looking Russian aristocracy that had become gripped by a passionate Francophilia. French tutors and governesses instructed the children of the upper classes, French physicians looked after their health, and French tailors and milliners told them what to wear if they wished—and they did wish—to obey the holy writ of Paris fashion. "Never," sighed Martha, "was a land so overrun with Locusts as this is with french."

French was also the language of gossip. Tales of financial ruin and disgrace at court were particularly popular subjects in the smartest drawing rooms. And to her horror, Martha learned that she herself had provided fodder for these wagging tongues: It was alleged that she had cultivated her elderly hostess's affections in a cold-hearted plot to alienate Dashkova from her own daughter, Madame Shcherbenin, with an eye to replacing her not only in the princess's heart but in her will. In fact, mother and daughter had fallen out with each other long before Martha came on the scene. Eventually Martha would discover that the source of the slander was Madame Shcherbenin herself.

Martha worried that the princess's "happiness appears to be linked with my stay," but, increasingly, she felt it was time to go home. Finally, in October 1808, despite the princess's pleadings, she bade her hostess a tearful farewell, and began the long westward journey. Her baggage contained all the gifts Dashkova had given her—a huge library of valuable and important books, boxes of jewelry and keepsakes, trunkfuls of new clothes, even a watch that had belonged to Peter the Great—that is, everything but Pashinka, the serf girl.

In Russia, the princess, perhaps pining for the young foreigner who meant more to her than her own daughter, survived little over a year after Martha's departure. She died in Moscow on January 4, 1810. In accordance with her last wishes, her body was taken back to Troitskoe for burial. Fittingly, the only mourners at her final rites were the local priest and a few serfs from the estate that had been her refuge and her delight.

On another estate, some 700 miles away from the grandeurs of Dashkova's Troitskoe, a landowner of a very different sort stirred behind the cheesecloth mosquito nets that curtained his wooden bed. Stepan Mikhailovich Bagrov yawned, scratched his broad chest with his callused hands, and emerged to greet the day. He slipped on a pair of stained leather shoes and stepped carefully over the bodies of the two menservants who still lay snoring on the floorboards. Wearing only the shirt he had slept in—a coarse linen garment woven by his peasants and given to him as part of their rent—he went out to sit on the top step of his small wooden porch and enjoy the breeze that wafted off the nearby river.

Bagrov, immortalized as Grandfather in the lightly fictionalized memoirs of the 19th-century writer Sergei Aksakov, contemplated his domain with quiet satisfaction. This nobleman had little in common, except his ownership of land, with the sophisticated grandees who wintered in their urban palaces and regarded their country mansions as summertime retreats. Moscow and St. Petersburg felt as foreign to Grandfather as Timbuktu, and he remained as firmly rooted on his own soil as the birches and rowans that shaded his millstream.

Everything he saw before him was the fruit of his own hard labor. In his youth, Grandfather had left the family estate near the Volga River, granted to his ancestors by royal decree many centuries before. By the time he came to manhood, the land—and the serfs to work it—had been parceled out among generations of male heirs and shaved off for daughters' dowries. The once ample water sources had shrunk to nothing, and too many squabbling proprietors struggled to extract a living from the same overexploited tract of ground.

So Grandfather had migrated eastward, to the still unspoiled Ufa province, a frontier territory of mountains, steppes, forests, and rich black soil. With him he brought dozens of families of serfs to help fell trees and work the land he had purchased on the banks of the fast-flowing Bolshoi Buguruslan River.

Now, savoring his morning tea from the steaming brass samovar, Grandfather watched the pigs rooting in his yard and greeted the cows that skirted the house on their leisurely parade from shed to pasture. After breakfast with his wife and children—five daughters and an infant son—he ordered his stableman, the barefoot Spiridon, to hitch a horse to the four-wheeled droshky and drive him around Bagrovo, as the estate was known.

Liveried serfs escort their masters, comfortably situated inside the carriage, on a trip between town and country. Landowners preferred winter travel, which was swift and smooth, and avoided journeys during the spring thaw, when wheels became mired in mud.

His tour of inspection took him past fields of oats, wheat, and rippling rye and along to the little patches where his peasants grew crops of their own. When they reached a fallow field, freshly plowed and ready for planting, Grandfather made Spiridon drive the droshky straight over the furrows to make sure the plowman had done his job properly. Luckily for the plowman, the soil had been tilled finely, with no telltale clumps of unworked earth to jar the droshky's wheels.

On the way home, Grandfather noted with interest that the strawberry bushes were just about ripe for picking. He made a mental note to send out the maids with their baskets, and brought home a handful of the first fruits to present to his wife, Arina.

The hot June day had done nothing to curb Grandfather's appetite. He rejoined his

Although serfs attached to country estates tended to specialize in particular jobs, not all were as busy as these workers engaged in various stages of barrelmaking. Some estates with many people to employ might have a serf whose chief duty was to light the lamps.

family for a lunch of hot cabbage soup followed by a second, iced soup made of beets and an assortment of fish dishes—fresh and salted sturgeon and a pile of crayfish gathered from the river, all washed down with copious drafts of cold home-brewed beer. To make sure the inevitable swarm of flies didn't spoil the master's dinner, a brawny manservant stood behind Grandfather's chair and brandished a birch branch to discourage the winged invaders.

After the sacred daily ritual of an afternoon nap and more beer and tea to wake him up again, Grandfather paid a visit to his mill and his poultry yard. Finally he spent an hour or so as a Slavic King Solomon, dispensing justice and arbitrating serfs' disputes.

This serf repairs a loom in his master's country estate. Landowners often had their serfs trained in various arts and crafts, making large estates culturally and economically self-sufficient.

Supper was as ample as lunch had been. To digest it in peace, Grandfather sent the rest of the family off to bed and sat alone on his porch, taking pleasure in the cool evening air and in the dim summer light that in those northern latitudes never faded from the sky until well past midnight.

All over Russia there were men like Grandfather, plain-spoken patriarchs of relatively modest means. They lived in comfort rather than princely luxury and didn't necessarily share the intellectual sophistication of Dashkova's circle. Grandfather himself was never much of a reader and found writing an effort, although no one could fault his arithmetical abilities, especially when it came to calculating profit and loss. Such provincial landlords stood several rungs below the urban grandees on the social ladder, and those who forgot their places were quickly reminded. One distinguished dowager, for instance, received highborn guests at the front door of her mansion, while those whose blood was a slightly paler shade of blue were promptly dispatched to the servants' entrance.

Another social vigilante, a rich magnate named Shipov, was known to adjust the warmth of his greeting according to the number of serfs possessed

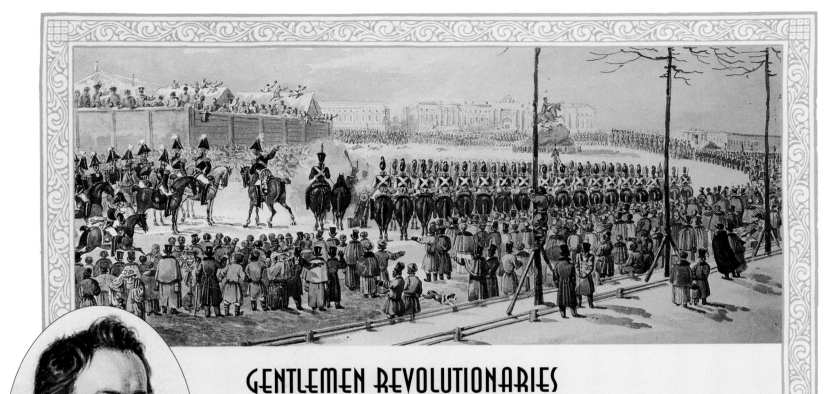

GENTLEMEN REVOLUTIONARIES

Inspired by the American and French Revolutions, a secret society of aristocratic army officers staged the abortive Decembrist uprising of 1825. Braving freezing temperatures, nearly 3,000 soldiers and sympathizers gathered at the statue of Peter the Great in St. Petersburg's Senate Square on the morning of December 14. They demanded an end to serfdom—calling it "our national disgrace"—and a constitution for their country. What they got instead was a calling-out of the imperial guard *(above)*, a brief but bloody confrontation, arrest, imprisonment, and exile.

In little over an hour, more than a thousand of the Decembrists were killed or wounded. Of the 120 leaders of the plot, the five found "the most guilty" were hanged and the rest banished to Siberia;

only a grant of amnesty in 1856 allowed their return to European Russia.

Additional sacrifices were made by the handful of women determined to join their banished husbands and fiancés in Siberia. Of the dozen or so women who made the journey, the youngest was 20-year-old Princess Maria Volkonskaya, shown at left with her husband, Sergei. Married for just a year when the uprising occurred, Maria risked the perils of a 4,000-mile trek—by sleigh in the middle of winter—to be with her husband during his imprisonment.

Then another tragedy befell the Volkonskys. Refused permission by the authorities to take her son, Nikolenka *(at left, with his mother)*, with her, Maria left him in the care of his grandmother in St. Petersburg. She never saw Nikolenka again. Soon after arriving in Siberia, she learned that the boy had died.

by the other party. Princess Dashkova, owner of thousands, could have counted on a deep bow and a warm smile, while Grandfather Bagrov, master of only 180 souls, would have had to content himself with the curtest of Shipov nods.

In some parts of the realm, the country estates of the great princes lay cheek by jowl with the holdings of the provincial gentry. But the grandees lived in neoclassical palaces adorned with grand staircases, massive porticoes, and domed pavilions; the Grandfather Bagrovs resided in low wooden houses, with rambling extensions or a modest mezzanine tacked on haphazardly as families grew.

Yet, though he sat on a tiny front porch surrounded by rooting pigs instead of on a marble terrace guarded by liveried servants, Grandfather Bagrov was content. Just as the tsar enjoyed absolute power over Russia, so Grandfather—like his male counterparts from the Baltic to Siberia—reigned supreme in his little domain. His spouse might hold sway over indoor servants and the mundane business of household management, but she was, at best, a mere lieutenant, the indoor equivalent of the overseer who governed the serfs in the fields.

Differences between the sexes were established early, and carefully fostered. "For boys," said one 19th-century educator, "the goal is the whole world, for girls—the home." Among the upper classes, adult men and women tended to spend more time apart than they did together. Many noble houses were divided into male and female zones, each staffed by servants of the appropriate gender. When large family groups went on a journey, men and women generally traveled separately. Separate never meant equal: The patriarch ruled, without sanctions, over his family as well as his serfs.

Inevitably, some landowners took advantage of their position. One notorious magnate named Koshkarov dispensed altogether with the inconveniences of married life. Instead, he provided himself with a harem of carefully selected and well-educated female serfs. Once they'd served their time with him, Koshkarov duly rewarded his ex-concubines by marrying them off to his lackeys.

In comparison, Grandfather seemed a fairly benign dictator. Still, living under his thumb, Arina Bagrov and her daughters protected themselves by studying his moods and caprices. The girls, unsurprisingly, grew up into master tacticians, good at fomenting domestic conspiracies. His only son, Alexei, perhaps seeking greater freedom than he'd ever get under Grandfather's roof, moved to the provincial capital, also called Ufa, to begin a career as a minor civil servant.

Then momentous news came to Bagrovo: Alexei had found himself a bride, a young woman named Sofia. Even on this great occasion, Grandfather refused to abandon his front porch and his home comforts for the rigors of a journey to town. So the drama of the proposal, the dowry negotiations, the details of the ceremony at the candlelit Church of the Dormition, and the round of parties and congratulatory visits were experienced only secondhand by Grandfather and Arina.

But Bagrovo did have its own part to play in the festivities. As important as the wedding itself was the newly married couple's first visit to the estate. The house was small, so the usual sleeping accommodations had to be reorganized. To provide a suitably festive nuptial chamber, one daughter was evicted from her pleasant room with its river view and transferred to a temporary couch in the bathhouse lobby. Then all her possessions were banished and replaced by a brand-new fourposter bed with luxurious curtains.

As Alexei and Sofia's carriage toiled up the hill and past the Bagrovo threshing barn, the whole estate exploded in a frenzy. Peasants, household servants, children, and hobbling elders assembled for a greeting ceremony in the courtyard in front of Grandfather's house.

Grandfather, dressed in a frock coat whose pomp was only slightly compromised by its antiquity, stood on the porch with

Arina beside him, resplendent in a silk shawl embroidered with golden threads. In their hands they held an icon of the Virgin, as well as a loaf of bread and a silver saltcellar, traditional symbols of prosperity and welcome. Bride and groom knelt to receive a blessing, then made a stately progress around every waiting family member, exchanging kisses. The village priest intoned prayers and sprinkled holy water.

Next, the young couple and the family went into the sitting room for an orgy of expensive gift giving. Meanwhile, mobs of peasants surged through the house to admire the honeymoon bed and the lavish dining table. They had to be shooed out to make room for the servants bringing in the feast. Grandfather's cook had risen to the occasion, pouring on the butter, cream, and spices with a generous hand.

After an extended stay at Bagrovo, punctuated by formal calls on all neighbors of suitable rank, the young pair went home to Ufa and settled down to the business of producing grandchildren for Stepan Mikhailovich. And when news of Sofia's pregnancy did reach him, Grandfather ordered the priest to hold a special church service to pray for the health of mother and child, then commemorated the great day by canceling some of the debts the peasants owed him and pouring drink down the throats of everyone he met.

The new arrival turned out to be a girl, and Grandfather shed few tears when the infant died. His heart was set on a boy. Finally, his prayers were answered. One day, an ecstatic messenger from Ufa burst in upon him during his afternoon nap to announce the arrival of baby Sergei. Grandfather, still half asleep, made the sign of the cross, then went to his tall chest of drawers, extracted the Bagrov family tree, and inscribed the name of the new addition inside a perfect circle.

Young Sergei, growing up in the bustling town of Ufa, would take little pleasure in his family's visits to the ancestral home. On one occasion, he and a younger sister had to spend a month with Grandfather when their own parents had business elsewhere. But inevitably there came the momentous day when all the clan was summoned to Bagrovo. Stepan Mikhailovich was dying.

Grandfather's last days, like those of any patriarch of his class, entailed their own particular set of gloomy rituals. The house was packed with relatives, every room and habitable outbuilding turned into a temporary campsite. The sounds of women's weeping came through the chinks in the wooden walls.

Six-year-old Sergei, along with his parents and sister, was allocated space in the drawing room, which was freezing because no one had thought to light the fire. The

In serf painter Mikhail Shibanov's *Celebrating the Marriage Contract,* family and friends gather around the bride and groom to rejoice in the happy occasion.

WORSHIP IN THE VILLAGE CHURCH

All across rural Russia, the hub of peasant life was the parish church. Most of these were simple wooden structures with a highly decorated iconostasis, or icon screen, as shown in the 19th-century church at right. The peasant faithful gathered in front of the screen, while the local landowner worshiped in a special area of the church.

The village priest usually was poor, like most of his parishioners, earning little for his services. To sustain himself and—since Orthodox priests could marry—his family, he would also tend a plot of land.

For the whole congregation, the culminating event in the church calendar year was the Easter celebration. As the faithful exchanged three kisses and swapped eggs, the country's traditional symbol of the Resurrection, they would call out to each other, *"Khristos Voskrese!"*– "Christ is risen!"

two children shivered on a small sofa while their father, Alexei, heir to Bagrovo, made do with a feather bed on the floor. It was a far cry from the expansive guest wing that the Wilmot sisters enjoyed at Troitskoe.

The vigil ran its course. There were summonses to the deathbed to receive Grandfather's wordless blessing, long days of hushed conversation, and a communal wailing from the entire household when the old man finally passed away. Priests arrived to read prayers. Grandfather, wrapped in a shroud, lay in state on the dining table.

On the day of the funeral, the coffin was borne by sleigh across the frozen ground to the nearby village churchyard, where Grandfather would be buried. A long procession of carriages and sleighs followed. Meanwhile, in Grandfather's empty bedroom, two men from the estate would spend the next eight days and nights reading psalms while a yellow candle burned before an icon. The climax of this period of mourning came on the ninth day, when all the generations of the clan gathered to pray for Grandfather's soul and celebrate his memory with a ceremonial feast.

Even Sergei noticed how the rest of the family now began to treat his own father differently: Alexei had become the patriarch. His sisters fell to their knees and begged him, "Be a father to us!" And Sofia turned, in an instant, from the somewhat alien, town-bred daughter-in-law into mistress of the house.

In due course, a provincial official would pay a visit, call the serfs together, and read out the ukase—the legal declaration giving Alexei Stepanovich full rights of ownership to Grandfather's estate. And young Sergei would find himself transported from the lively streets of Ufa to the wooded banks of the Bolshoi Buguruslan River, as the new heir apparent of Bagrovo.

Sergei Bagrov—the fictional alter ego of writer Sergei Aksakov himself—faced a future as a country landlord whether he wanted it or not. His life would be circumscribed by the rigid social conventions of the class into which he was born. Yet these constraints paled into insignificance in comparison with the plight of one of Aksakov's own friends and colleagues, the celebrated actor Mikhail Shchepkin.

Shchepkin was born in 1788 in Ukraine, on the estate of a noble family known as Wolkenstein. Some 45 years before Shchepkin's birth, his great-grandfather had served as a priest in a rural church located near the Wolkensteins' country mansion; the cleric's 13-year-old son, Grigory, sang in the church choir. When Count Wolkenstein attended the service one Sunday morning, he became so captivated by the youth's angelic voice that he forced Grigory to become his serf. The choirboy and his descendants would remain, in perpetuity, the property of the Wolkensteins.

Mikhail was the product of an unromantic serf marriage. In accordance with an old tradition, the Count Wolkenstein of the day had paired off his valet—Semyon, son of the enslaved chorister—with Marie, the maid who served his own new bride.

Mikhail's parents belonged to the most privileged class of serfs, far removed from the toilers in the fields. From this elite came trusted family attendants, living and working in close proximity to their masters. As stewards and overseers, they occupied positions of authority over their fellows.

And the serfs who showed musical or dramatic talent were recruited as performers in the private theaters that so many aristocrats—Princess Dashkova among them—had created on their estates. Some, like the troupe who entertained the Wilmots at Troitskoe, might serve both the Muses and the dinner in the course of a single evening; others were allowed to concentrate only on their art.

The Shchepkin family's master, Count Wolkenstein, had a theater too. It was housed in a large hall, with a canvas proscenium arch and a striped curtain separating the narrow trestle-mounted stage from the three rows of seats. When little Mikhail, aged eight, was allowed in to witness a comic opera called *The New Family,* he was dazzled by what he saw. "I didn't realize," commented the actor long afterward, "that the evening was to determine my entire future."

On the night in question, Mikhail was preparing to begin his formal schooling. His parents, with the master's consent, were determined to give their son the best possible education. Soon thereafter, he made his own triumphant dramatic debut in a class play. His course was set.

At secondary school in the town of Kursk in southern Russia, Shchepkin's excellent memory not only helped him earn high grades and the enthusiastic support of his teachers but also won him entry to a theatrical company. The troupe was composed of serf performers owned by several local landowners.

The young actor soon found himself living a life fraught with contradictions. He basked in the applause of Kursk audiences and socialized with school friends who were the scions of local noble families. But he was never allowed to forget his serf status: Whenever the count gave a ball or banquet, he ordered Shchepkin home to take the coats or pour the wine. And if the count himself didn't require Mikhail's services, the nobleman would allow his aristocratic friends to hire the boy as a temporary waiter.

Count Nicholas Sheremetev was the wealthiest man in all Russia, and his country estate at Ostankino, shown below, was its most elaborate showplace for the arts. He owned two million acres of land in 17 provinces and maintained 210,000 serfs, one of whom became his wife.

THE GLORIES OF OSTANKINO

In the spring of 1797, Count Nicholas Sheremetev welcomed Emperor Paul I, son of Catherine the Great, to his country estate with a spectacular display. The count stationed a serf next to every tree in the grove that led to the estate; each of the trees had been sawed nearly all the way through. As the emperor's entourage made their way up the long drive, the trees fell away on signal. To the visiting tsar, it was as if a curtain were opening, and there before him, set off by a tremendous fireworks display, stood the glories of Ostankino—its church, pond, gardens, and the magnificent palace itself.

Designed by the top architects of the day, the palace at Ostankino, just north of Moscow, boasted the most splendid and elaborate private theater in Russia. Ostankino's theater company numbered 230 serf actors, dancers, singers, musicians, wardrobe mistresses, scenic artists, and wigmakers, all trained in Sheremetev's own academy of theatrical arts.

In his patronage of the arts, Count Sheremetev was supported by his wife, Praskovya, who had, in fact, been one of the family's serf performers. At age seven, the girl had become part of the Sheremetev household, where she learned various lan-

When this portrait was painted, the pregnant Countess Sheremetev was already ill. Around her neck she wears her husband's image on a medallion.

guages and took up music and singing. Four years later, she made her debut in the large serf theater at Kuskovo, another Sheremetev estate, and eventually became one of the count's star sopranos. Nicholas referred to his troupe of ballerinas and singers as the "girls in my house" and gave each the name of a precious gemstone. He fell in love with Praskovya, "the Pearl," and after an affair, they were secretly married in a small parish church in 1801.

But the couple's happiness was destined to be short lived. Praskovya survived only long enough to bear the count a son before she died of tuberculosis early in 1803. After she passed away, Count Nicholas lost all interest in the theater, and within six years he was dead too.

By lowering its parquet floor five feet—a mechanical operation that took less than an hour—Ostankino's ballroom was converted into a theater that seated 250. The room, seen here from the stage, rivaled the best theaters of Europe. Performances were rendered particularly thrilling by the flying machines, trapdoors, magic lanterns, and other special effects devised by a skilled serf carpenter.

After Mikhail's schooling ended, the count allowed Mikhail to continue his acting career, but also insisted that he train as a land surveyor for service on the estate. Thus for several years, Shchepkin's life swung between the seasonal poles of rural estate work and provincial theater.

In 1810 the 22-year-old actor fell in love with a young woman named Elena Dmitrieva. Her status was shadowy—she'd been taken into an aristocratic family as a foundling and become the ward of the princess Salagova. In her youth she had been more or less abandoned by her patron and compelled to earn her living as a seamstress. Marriage to Shchepkin would, by law, make her the Wolkensteins' serf; she announced that she would willingly give up her freedom for his sake.

In 1816, after Count Wolkenstein had passed away, Shchepkin was invited to join a theater company in the university town of Kharkov. It was a tantalizing offer; Kharkov would give him a much larger audience for his talents. But he couldn't move without the widowed countess's permission, which she eventually gave him.

Two years later, he was approached by Prince Repnin, an aristocratic impresario with lofty artistic ambitions, who sought to recruit Shchepkin for his private theater on his estate at Poltava. The countess agreed to lend her land surveyor to Prince

Repnin, "with my most humble request that when I need him, he will then be sent back to me." Shchepkin's growing body of admirers went a step further; they petitioned the Wolkensteins to grant the actor his freedom. His talents, they asserted, would never flourish if he remained enslaved.

The countess agreed to let Mikhail Shchepkin buy his own freedom as well as that of his wife and children. The actor did not have enough money, however, and he instead permitted Prince Repnin to purchase him and his family. The prince paid his actors—even serfs—an annual salary and sent them out on tours of the provinces. As Mikhail Shchepkin traveled throughout Russia, he acquired thousands of additional fans, and he hoarded every ruble that he earned in the hope that one day he

the last of the old bonds broken, Shchepkin was now free to move his family to Moscow, and there he became one of the best-known and best-loved actors in the Russian theater.

Shchepkin's talent bought freedom for himself and his family. But few of his fellow serfs, whatever their inborn gifts, had that opportunity to break their chains. The vast majority were peasants, most of whom were illiterate, and they were tied, by law, to their masters' estates.

Every estate was its own little absolute monarchy. On all but the smallest properties, masters and peasants had few occasions for direct contact. Stewards and overseers, generally serfs themselves, passed down the orders from on high.

"God is in His Heaven, and the Tsar is far away."

would be able to buy his household's freedom from the prince.

In 1822 a job offer from a large theater company in the city of Tula, not far from Moscow, brought with it enough money for the now famous Shchepkin to free himself, Elena, and their two eldest children. But he was still 4,000 rubles short of the price Prince Repnin demanded for the freedom of Shchepkin's parents, his siblings, and his two youngest children. With expectations of substantial earnings, he offered the prince a promissory note to cover the sum. But his new celebrity status counted for nothing: His ex-master turned him down. A newly freed serf, jeered Repnin, was hardly creditworthy.

Eventually, one of Shchepkin's longstanding admirers came to the rescue and offered himself as Shchepkin's financial guarantor. At this, the prince agreed to grant the family liberty. With

Some nobles displayed a genuine concern for their serfs' well-being; others were sadists, notorious for the physical and mental torments they inflicted. In theory, the law prevented nobles from murdering their peasants outright or from breaking up serf families. But no legislation stopped a lord from ordering a flogging that just happened to be long and hard enough to kill. Victims of despotic masters were on their own, with no expectation of help from higher powers. "God," they lamented, "is in His Heaven, and the Tsar is far away."

The institution of serfdom had prevailed throughout Russia since the reign of Ivan the Terrible in the 1500s, and as the tsars' dominions expanded through treaty, conquest, and colonization, millions of formerly free peasants found themselves under the yoke. By giving the nobility the ownership of their peasants, the tsars cemented the bond between the throne and the aristocracy.

In essence, the relationship between master and serf resembled an unwritten contract between two parties. Yet from the peasant's point of view, there was nothing voluntary or negotiable about it. The landowner provided protection and shelter: logs to build a house, clothes or the raw materials to make them, and protection from starvation in times of famine. In exchange, the serf owed the landlord rent, physical labor, or a combination of the two—and his freedom.

Peasants' lives were arduous, ruled by the demands of the soil and the seasons. There were, however, pleasures and diversions—feast days, trips to fairs and markets, weddings, baptisms, all the communality of close-knit family and village life. During this seasonal round, the Orthodox Church imposed a moral framework and a ritual calendar, but the old pagan spirits of the forest had never been totally exiled. Magic might be called upon to affect the outcome of a love affair; folk remedies, sometimes supplemented by a spell, were relied upon to cure most ills.

Even in the late 18th century, the golden age of the Russian country estate, many serfs' lives were far from the pastoral idyll depicted by the artists whose works hung on the mansion walls. But in the 1800s the landowning classes began to come under increasing

Known for the naturalness of his performances, serf actor Mikhail Shchepkin *(on the left)* strikes a formal pose in this portrait with a fellow actor.

economic pressure, which inevitably translated itself into heavier demands on their serfs.

The gap between rich and poor yawned wider than ever before. Some previously wealthy nobles faced ruin. The first stirrings of industrialization and a market economy were at least partially responsible. Some districts also suffered long spells of disappointing crops or actual famine. But there were also many landlords who had long lived beyond their means and now paid the price for years—or generations—of financial fecklessness.

Some proprietors raised cash by selling or mortgaging their serfs and their land, and peasants often found themselves at the mercy of new owners who were eager to extract as much profit as possible from the land and from those who worked it. Twenty percent of the serfs owned by the nobility in 1820 had been mortgaged to the Nobles' Land Bank, a state credit institution; by 1859 this figure had risen to 66 percent.

The serfs themselves began to abandon their customary fatalism. No longer did they passively accept their oppression as the will of God and tsar. By the 1820s there were rumblings, small localized revolts, but these uprisings were large enough to reverberate as far as St. Petersburg and make the government stir uneasily in its gilded chairs. Between 1826 and 1829,

Though they now could serve on local councils, or zemstvos, alongside their former masters, the lives of Russia's peasants changed little after they were liberated from serfdom in 1861 by Alexander II *(inset)*. In the painting at far right, *The Zemstvo at Dinner,* peasants eat bread and onions in the street while the aristocrats, unseen, dine inside.

angry serfs caused 85 significant disturbances; between 1845 and 1849, the number swelled to 207.

The peasants found allies first among the intelligentsia. The westward-looking educated classes had begun to find the whole system of serfdom untenable. Not only was it morally reprehensible and economically backward, but it also showed up Russia as a barbarous society. Even members of the landed gentry whose comfortable lifestyles rode on the bowed shoulders of their serfs began to question their own class's entitlement to hold such power over fellow human beings.

By 1856 the tsar himself acknowledged that the old order deserved to die. In an address to the landed gentry of Moscow province he declared: "You yourselves know that the existing order of ruling over living souls cannot remain unchanged. It is better to abolish serfdom from above than to await the day when it will begin to abolish itself from below."

It would take five years of debates, negotiations, infighting, mathematical wrangling, and reluctant compromise before Alexander II achieved what he set out to do. On March 3, 1861, he issued his Emancipation Act.

In the cities, intellectuals gathered to express their satisfaction. In an elegant drawing room, a pious lady, whose name has been lost, wrote in her journal and gave thanks that "a centuries-old sin weighing on the nobility's conscience has been absolved, and our terrible responsibility before God lifted from us."

Perhaps on the same day, on the estate belonging to Shchepkin's old masters, the Wolkensteins, a crowd of peasants surrounded an elderly neighbor. In his youth he might have been one of the serf artisans who produced the plays at the old count's private theater. He might even have known the great Shchepkin himself. And, unlike the farm hands and dairymaids who clustered around him, he knew how to read. So it fell to him, in a voice that trembled with emotion, to read the tsar's own words, announcing to his listeners that they were serfs no longer. The old order was dead.

BOUND TO THE LAND

Spring casts its soft light over a typical Russian village in a painting dating from 1840 *(right)* that shows the villagers celebrating Whitsunday. Constituting more than 80 percent of the country's population, Russia's peasants often lived their entire lives in simple towns like this one, laid out along a river and having but a single, unpaved street, dominated by a domed church.

Before Alexander II abolished serfdom in 1861, privately owned peasants fell into two categories: those bound to the master and those bound to the land. Unlike serfs bound to a master, serfs attached to the land could not be sold. Because they worked the same fields year in and year out, they would say to their masters, "We are yours, but the land is ours."

The agricultural cycle determined the rhythm of life, with the warm months given to field labor and the long, cold winter to producing woven or carved wooden items that were sold for much-needed cash. Frequent religious holidays helped break the monotony, and generosity characterized country hospitality. "The house," it was said, "is not made beautiful by its rooms but by its pies."

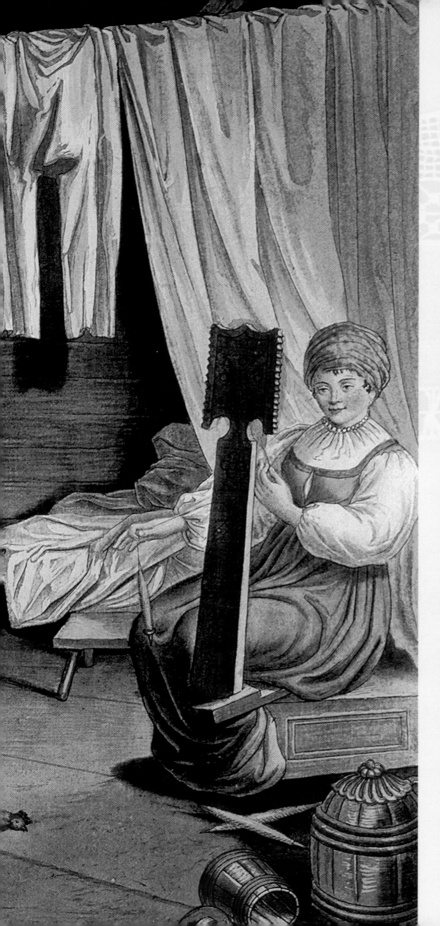

AT HOME

Chickens and a cat share the living area of a typical wooden house with a bearded farmer and his industrious wife, as portrayed in a colored lithograph from 1821. The man sits close to the oven for warmth. His seat is a wooden bench that in most peasant dwellings ran around three walls; when spread with furs at night, it doubled as a bed. On his feet he wears bast shoes, made from the plaited inner bark of the lime tree, with strips of cloth wound around his lower legs for insulation. Easily made, bast shoes were noted for their comfort and had the further advantage of not retaining moisture.

The wife is busy with her wooden distaff, spinning thread from flax she grew, then processed and carefully carded. She will use the thread to weave linen cloth. Dyed blue, her cloth might wind up as baggy trousers or a jacket for her husband or as a *sarafan,* a sleeveless overdress, for herself. White linen would become aprons and chemises. So closely associated was the distaff with women's work that it served as a symbol of Russian womanhood; a ritual distaff sometimes was used to sever the umbilical cords of newborn girls.

This distaff, with attached seat, consists of a decorated upper portion, or blade, whose comblike top held carded flax or wool. Russian women preferred the distaff to the spinning wheel because it could be carried easily to neighbors' homes for communal spinning.

A DOWN-TO-EARTH FAITH

The arrival of a miracle-working icon brings an entire village to this humble spot to gaze upon the image of the Madonna and child in an 1878 masterpiece by Konstantin Savitsky, *Bringing Out an Icon to the People.* As a bearded prelate alights from his carriage assisted by two black-robed priests, many villagers, garbed in their finest, have already dropped to their knees.

Faith played an important role in the daily lives of the Russian peasants. Every home, no matter how humble, featured a "beautiful corner," where the family icon took pride of place. A foreign traveler who had broken bread at a rough-hewn peasant table observed that her hosts saluted their icons "with the sign of the cross and a murmured prayer" at the start and end of every meal.

Most peasants were illiterate, but icons at home and in the churches provided visual "texts" they could understand. And parents who were able taught their children how to read from the family's single book, the Bible.

The items placed in the "beautiful corner" of a restored peasant home reveal a humble grace: the draped icon, the embroidered cloths at the windows, and a traditional bird-shaped vessel called a *kovsh.*

91

A FESTIVE SPIRIT

Russian peasants loved festive occasions, and the church calendar was filled with religious holidays that gave them numerous opportunities for celebration. The painting at left depicts such an event, in which a couple dances with wild abandon while local musicians play and guests look on happily, dressed in their best hand-stitched clothing.

Holidays offered not only a respite from labor, they were also an excuse for a grand party at which the many invited guests ate well and drank hard. "Besides the relatives," wrote a Russian-born author recalling the feasts of his childhood, "there were friends, pilgrims, neighbors, and beggars, 'sent by the Lord.' "

An old proverb says, "Bring to the table everything you can find in the oven," but most Russian hosts did not need to be reminded to be generous, even though they were poor. Indeed, the Russian word for hospitality, *khlebosolstvo,* derives from *khleb* and *sol,* or bread and salt, the humblest of foods.

The ceramic pitcher below held *kvas,* a popular fermented drink made from barley, honey, and salt. Ice inserted into the hole kept the beverage cool.

CHAPTER THREE

"WE CAN NO LONGER LIVE LIKE THIS"

Nicholas II and his bride, Alexandra, pose in the garden at Tsarskoe Selo soon after their marriage in 1894. The ill-prepared tsar was 26 when he succeeded to the throne, his German-born tsarina just 22. "I weep and worry all day long," Alexandra confided to a friend, "because I feel that my husband is so young and so inexperienced."

To history he would be known as the Tsar-Liberator, the man responsible for freeing the serfs and carrying out sweeping domestic reform. But to the small but determined revolutionary groups of late-19th-century Russia, Alexander II was a symbol of repression whose death was necessary to bring about a new order.

The most radical of these groups was the People's Will, founded in St. Petersburg in June 1879. Six times its members had tried—and failed—to kill the tsar. They had tried in Odessa, Moscow, Kharkov, and St. Petersburg. Early in 1881 they were ready to try again.

On the morning of Sunday, March 13, Alexander and his entourage of mounted Cossack guards made their way through the quiet streets of St. Petersburg. Riding inside his enclosed carriage, the tsar probably didn't see the young woman who waved her handkerchief as he approached. But at that prearranged signal, one of the woman's comrades stepped forward and hurled a bomb at the royal carriage. The explosion brought down some horses and guardsmen, but it only damaged the heavy carriage.

The 63-year-old tsar was unharmed. It was then, however, that he made a fatal mistake: He stepped down onto the street to assist the wounded. Seeing his opportunity, a second man closed to within six feet and threw another bomb directly at Alexander. The bomb exploded at the tsar's feet, fatally ripping away his legs and lacerating his body and face.

"I'm cold, so cold," Alexander whispered as an aide bent to cover him with a cloak. "Take me to the Palace . . . to die."

The People's Will had succeeded. Nine days later its leaders sent a letter to Alexander's son and heir, who had by then already been proclaimed Alexander III. After apologizing for intruding on his grief, the group suggested that there were two courses open to the new tsar: either repression and the inevitable revolution, or a "voluntary turning to the people on the part of the Supreme Authority." The letter closed by saying, "And now, Your Majesty, decide."

His Majesty wasted no time. He chose the *nagaika,* the Cossack whip—and, ultimately, revolution. The reign of Alexander III was one of reaction and repression. When he died of kidney disease at the age of 49, he was succeeded by his son, Nicholas II. Nicholas's troubled reign would last until 1917, when he would enter history as the last of the Russian tsars.

It was unthinkable that the ruler of all Russia should not be married. And so on November 26, 1894, one week after his father had been laid to rest, Nicholas Alexandrovich Romanov took as his wife and empress a beautiful young woman with lines to the greatest royal families of Europe. She was 22-year-old Princess Alix of Hesse, the daughter of a German grand duke as well as a granddaughter of England's Queen Victoria. A more suitable consort could scarcely have been found. But to the intensely superstitious Russians, Alexandra, as she would be called, had entered Russia as a "bird of ill-omen."

The first the public saw of their tsarina-to-be was at Alexander III's funeral, when she rode, alone and heavily veiled, in a carriage apart from the rest of the family. Old women along the route crossed themselves and whispered, "She has come to us behind a coffin." Alexandra herself could not help but feel the weight of the situation. Her wedding ceremony was subdued, a private affair; because of the national mourning, there could be no reception and no honeymoon. "Our marriage," she wrote her sister, "seemed to me a mere continuation of the masses for the dead with this difference, that now I wore a white dress instead of a black."

Yet there was no suppressing the joy she felt over her new husband. The two had been in love for some years, and their union would remain strong to the end of their lives. On her wedding night, she wrote in her husband's diary: "At last united, bound for life, and when this life is ended, we meet again in the other world and remain together for eternity. Yours, Yours." In the morning she penned: "Never did I believe there could be such utter happiness in this world, such a feeling of unity between two mortal beings. I love you, those three words have my life in them."

Nicholas worshiped her in return. But she was the only delight in his new life, for a less likely monarch would be hard to imagine. Nicholas II did not look like a tsar, did not act like a tsar, did not enjoy being tsar. "What am I going to do," he had wept at his father's death. "I am not prepared to be a Tsar. I never wanted to become one. I know nothing of the business of ruling. I have no idea of even how to talk to the ministers."

His father had been tall, as robust as a Russian bear, commanding; the son was short, slight, wishing to be liked, diffident to the point of once queuing up to dance with a favorite princess at a ball. "His Majesty goes too far in his modesty," remarked a tactful friend.

Others were less kind. They saw in Nicholas an irresolute "paralysis of will," as one of them put it, that led the young tsar to follow whoever spoke with him last. That was not quite true; Nicholas was reasonably intelligent and actually quite stubborn in his beliefs. But he so disliked saying no that he often remained silent—which the petitioner took for assent, only to regard Nicholas as either spineless or perfidious when matters turned out differently.

Added to this unfortunate mix were four loudmouthed, bullying uncles and a domineering mother, 47-year-old Dowager Empress Marie, who was determined to remain center stage. Nicholas propitiated them all and, on more than one occasion, responded to a tough question by saying, "I shall ask my mother."

A year passed in domestic bliss and imperial misery. "Along with this irreparable woe, the Lord has rewarded me with unimaginable happiness by giving me Alix," Nicholas wrote in his diary. A daughter, Olga, the first of four, was born in November and announced to St. Petersburg with a 101-gun salute; there would have been 300 guns for a son. Bursting with maternal love, Alexandra nursed, bathed, and cared for her infant herself, while Nicholas barely made it through the daily duties of state before hurrying back to his family.

At last the mourning period for Alexander III was over, and on May 26, 1896, Russia celebrated the new tsar's coronation. The five-hour ceremony in Moscow's candlelit Cathedral of the Assumption included a mass followed by prayers; by Nicholas swearing to rule as "Emperor and Autocrat of All the Russias"; and by Nicholas receiving the sacraments of the church.

Then came the omen.

As Nicholas stood on the steps of the altar, the heavy chain collar of the Order of St. Andrew slipped from his shoulders and fell clattering to the floor. An attendant reattached the collar so swiftly that only those nearby realized what had happened. They were sworn to deepest secrecy lest word of the incident get out, but all who were

This heavy silver-and-diamond collar of the Order of St. Andrew fell from Nicholas's shoulders during his coronation ceremony. Equally troublesome was the nine-pound imperial crown *(top),* which pressed on a scar on the tsar's forehead and gave him a headache.

there probably wondered what the ominous portent would mean for the new sovereign.

Nicholas went on with the ceremony. He picked up the imperial crown, which had been designed in 1762 for Catherine the Great. Carefully he placed the crown on his head, then removed it and tenderly put it on Alexandra's head for a moment before placing it back on his own.

For Nicholas, the coronation was a service of profound religious communion, binding together God, the tsar, and the Orthodox people. His character would not change; he would remain hesitant, diffident, largely ineffective, still reluctant and hating the business of ruling. But this naturally pious young man now believed that he had assumed before God a responsibility for Russia that God alone could relieve him of.

The next day, by tradition, the emperor and empress would celebrate among the people at an enormous outdoor festival. Each member of the assembled crowd would be given free food and beer and a little present as a souvenir of the occasion—porcelain cups stamped with the double-headed Romanov eagle for the men, similarly marked kerchiefs for the women.

The site was the Khodynka Field, a military training ground just outside the city. By early morning, more than half a million people had gathered there, everyone hoping for a look at the new tsar and tsarina and waiting for the 10:00 a.m. distribution of refreshments and souvenirs. Suddenly a rumor—hideously false, as it happened—swept the crowd: There was not enough beer, and only the first to come would get any. The crowd surged forward, people in the rear shoving, shouldering, kicking those ahead. A thin line of mounted Cossacks barred the way, but the mob swept on like a tidal wave, literally lifting the soldiers' horses into the air. By the hundreds, then by the thousands, men, women, and children stumbled and fell to the ground. Cossack reinforcements arrived swiftly. But by the time they had the mob under control, at least 1,300 people had been trampled to death and more than 10,000 were injured.

Nicholas and Alexandra were overwhelmed with horror and grief. The young tsar's first impulse was to rush to the scene, but his mother and his uncles dissuaded him; he must not be associated with tragedy. Instead, they persuaded Nicholas to do something that would forever color his subjects' view of their monarch.

The French ambassador had planned an elaborate ball for that evening. Nicholas and Alexandra did not wish to go, but Nicholas's uncles and ministers—fearful of offending the French—insisted that he attend. He and Alexandra did so, somberly, and spent

the next days visiting the injured in hospitals throughout Moscow. But all that many Russians would remember was their newly crowned tsar and his "German woman" heartlessly dancing away the day on which so many of their subjects had died. Shortly thereafter, while the tsar was at Nizhni Novgorod inaugurating the first great exhibition of Russian industry, a hailstorm of unprecedented ferocity disrupted the event. Sinister omens were piling on sinister omens.

As at the start of every reign, the new tsar was besieged with all manner of petitions. The ones that concerned Nicholas and his advisers most were from the numerous local elected councils, or zemstvos, created by Alexander II but later weakened by his son, Alexander III. Though largely dominated by the aristocracy, the councils nevertheless brought doctors, veterinarians, teachers, agronomists—all the educated men of Russia's provinces—into the governmental process. And these people hoped for the establishment of a central parliament.

Their answer had come on January 17, 1895, at a gathering of zemstvo delegates to greet the young emperor. Nicholas began nervously in a high falsetto: "Recently at certain meetings of local councils we have heard the voices of people carried away by senseless dreams of participation by zemstvo representatives in internal government." Then his voice swelled, and he finished in a virtual bellow: "Let it be known to all that I shall devote all my strength, for the good of the whole nation, to maintaining the principle of autocracy just as firmly and unflinchingly as it was preserved by my unforgettable dead father."

The emperor's sudden shout startled an elderly delegate

holding a golden tray with the traditional good-luck offering of bread and salt. The tray clattered to the floor, spilling everything. In embarrassment, Nicholas attempted to pick it up, but a court minister got there first—amid a dour shaking of heads over this unhappy sign.

The statement crushing zemstvo hopes was a clear indication that this tsar, on all issues of sovereignty, was a Romanov autocrat to the core. As a boy, Nicholas had idolized his father. Alexander did not return the love, but rather, perhaps because of his son's slender frame and docile manner, called him "girlie" and "dunce." Nevertheless Nicholas grew up believing implicitly in everything his father stood for, most particularly in the notion of the tsar as the embodiment of God on earth. According to Count Sergei Witte, Nicholas's finance minister and one of the few enlightened men in government, the young monarch believed that "people do not influence events, that God directs everything, and that the Tsar, as God's anointed, should not take advice from anyone but follow only his divine inspiration."

Such an attitude, set against a background of repression and rising ferment, would in all likelihood have made it impossible for even a tsar of genius and charisma to rule successfully. Nicholas displayed neither of these qualities. And his belief in divine inspiration derived in large part from his mother, his uncles, and advisers who regarded every liberal thought as treasonous.

The repressive reactionism of Alexander III's regime continued unimpeded under Nicholas. The press was supervised strictly; the powers of zemstvos were curtailed;

non-Orthodox believers and minorities, especially the Jews, were persecuted. As a result, angry demonstrations against the tsar and his regime flared in the countryside and cities. In February 1901 the minister of education was assassinated, and two months later, the minister of internal affairs. Nicholas reacted by appointing as his new internal affairs minister Vyacheslav Plehve, a hard-hearted policeman who had made his name hunting down the killers of Alexander II. He would not enjoy a long life, but would himself succumb to a bomb in July 1904. The frightful cycle of repression and revenge continued.

The tsar's conduct of foreign affairs proved no less appalling. In February 1904 war broke out in the Far East between Russia and Japan, both of whom coveted Manchuria and Korea. The conflict brought an early outpouring of patriotism from all sections of Russian society, and for a time ruler and ruled were united. Although Nicholas himself yearned to be at the front sharing the "danger and privations of the army," he remained at home, reviewing the troops and passing out little icons to soldiers going off to war. Alexandra turned the Winter Palace's grand salons into workrooms where she and the noble ladies of St. Petersburg made bandages, mittens, and socks for the wounded.

But after a series of humiliating Russian defeats, popular support for the war evaporated. Only the peace brokered by the American president, Theodore Roosevelt, preserved any honor for Russia. Although the treaty acknowledged Japan's para-

A cartoon of a Russian ogre about to devour a tiny Japanese soldier depicts the expected outcome of the war when it began in 1904. Russia's army numbered three million men, Japan's just 600,000.

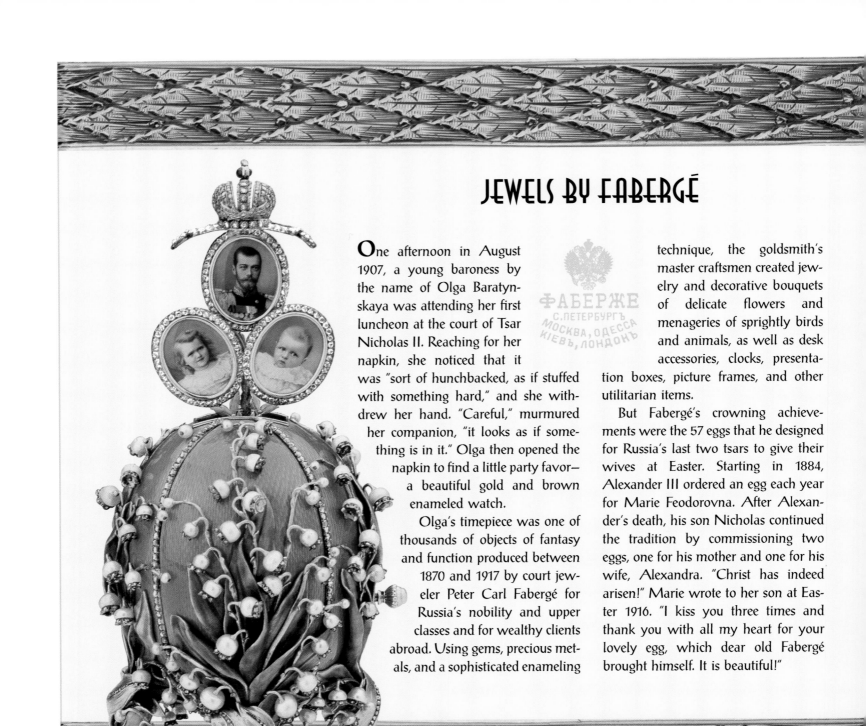

JEWELS BY FABERGÉ

One afternoon in August 1907, a young baroness by the name of Olga Baratynskaya was attending her first luncheon at the court of Tsar Nicholas II. Reaching for her napkin, she noticed that it was "sort of hunchbacked, as if stuffed with something hard," and she withdrew her hand. "Careful," murmured her companion, "it looks as if something is in it." Olga then opened the napkin to find a little party favor— a beautiful gold and brown enameled watch.

Olga's timepiece was one of thousands of objects of fantasy and function produced between 1870 and 1917 by court jeweler Peter Carl Fabergé for Russia's nobility and upper classes and for wealthy clients abroad. Using gems, precious metals, and a sophisticated enameling technique, the goldsmith's master craftsmen created jewelry and decorative bouquets of delicate flowers and menageries of sprightly birds and animals, as well as desk accessories, clocks, presentation boxes, picture frames, and other utilitarian items.

But Fabergé's crowning achievements were the 57 eggs that he designed for Russia's last two tsars to give their wives at Easter. Starting in 1884, Alexander III ordered an egg each year for Marie Feodorovna. After Alexander's death, his son Nicholas continued the tradition by commissioning two eggs, one for his mother and one for his wife, Alexandra. "Christ has indeed arisen!" Marie wrote to her son at Easter 1916. "I kiss you three times and thank you with all my heart for your lovely egg, which dear old Fabergé brought himself. It is beautiful!"

Nicholas gave this pink enamel egg encrusted with pearl lilies of the valley to his mother at Easter in 1898. The portraits of the tsar and his oldest daughters popped up at the turn of a knob.

A miniature watch of lavender enamel, gold, and diamonds hangs from a brooch depicting the head of an elephant.

This delicately enameled case once contained personal calling cards. Its gold borders are studded with pearls.

Brilliant blue enamel cornflowers with diamond stamens and gold buds stand in a rock crystal vase.

Double-headed Romanov eagles, a diamond crown, and a diamond Cyrillic letter *N* for Nicholas adorn this enamel-and-gold box.

A carved green nephrite frog with rose diamond eyes perches atop a gold parasol handle.

Troops open fire on civilians outside the Winter Palace on Bloody Sunday, January 22, 1905. The protesters had hoped to petition the tsar for a minimum wage and an eight-hour workday.

mount interest in Korea and agreed to restore Manchuria to China, Russia retained all its Far Eastern possessions and remained a great power in the Pacific. Back home, however, the old order was unraveling.

The year 1905 began with a calamity that forever destroyed the image of the Tsar-Batyushka, the loving and beloved Little Father from whom only good things flowed. On Sunday morning, January 22, a crowd of 150,000 men, women, and children marched to the Winter Palace to petition Nicholas for a wide range of reforms. Their leader, a radical priest named Georgy Gapon, had convinced them that the tsar was obliged before God to satisfy their demands if they, "the people," went directly to him. And so they went, dressed in their best, singing hymns and holding up icons and pictures of Nicholas.

Troops met them in the square before the palace. Taken aback by the size of the crowd, the jittery soldiers fired two warning volleys into the air and then started shooting into the advancing mass. That day, Bloody Sunday, as it would be known, about 100 marchers were slain, hundreds more wounded—and among the people, the mood changed from disbelief to anger. "I saw these looks of hatred and vengeance on literally every face—old and young, men and women," recalled an observer. "The revolution had truly been born."

The revolution of 1905 *had* been born. Throughout the winter, walkouts crippled factories across Russia. At Moscow University, 3,000 students burned a portrait of the tsar and festooned the buildings with red flags; student unrest soon reached the point at which the government closed virtually all centers of higher learning. Intellectuals everywhere voiced outrage and demanded reform. The zemstvos renewed their campaign for representative government through a freely elected constituent assembly. Professional groups—doctors, lawyers, teachers, engineers—started organizing at the national level and combining into a Union of Unions. They were joined by a Women's Union for Equality and by unions of clerks, bookkeepers, and railway workers. The press bannered all their grievances, and when a leading paper proclaimed, "We can no longer live like this," the poignant phrase swept the nation.

Waves of rebellion rolled through the countryside. Peasants went on strike against the landowners. They felled the gentry's trees, cut their hay, stole their livestock, appropriated their tools. In early summer, peasant mobs invaded, looted, and burned the manor houses; flames lit the night sky and silhouetted lines of horse-drawn carts filled with plundered paintings and statues, antique furniture, Oriental rugs, crystal, porcelain, silks, and satins. In all, nearly 3,000 manors were destroyed.

The government sent troops to quell the uprisings—no fewer than 2,700 times from January to October. But the ordinary soldiers were peasants themselves and deeply sympathetic to their fellows, and whole units rebelled and refused to carry out orders.

Nicholas remained oblivious to the gravity of the situation. It was easy for his advisers to convince him that "foreign revolutionaries" had been responsible for Bloody Sunday. And when in September strikes broke out all across the country, Nicholas spent most of his time hunting. "The Tsar," remarked a courtier, "is living in an utter fool's paradise, thinking that He is as strong and all-powerful as before." On October 9, Sergei Witte, now serving as prime minister, bluntly told Nicholas that there were two choices open to him. He could establish a military dictatorship. Or, as Witte himself favored, he could grant the people civil liberties and set up a constitutional government with a legislative Duma, or central parliament, elected on a democratic franchise.

Not surprisingly, Nicholas chose dictatorship, turning to his uncle, Grand Duke Nicholas, to assume the role of dictator. But the older man had grasped the reality: With a roar, he whipped out his revolver and threatened suicide then and there if the tsar did not endorse Witte's plan. At that, his nephew conceded defeat.

The proclamation of the October Manifesto on October 30 was greeted with joy in St. Petersburg. The martyrs of Bloody Sunday had won after all. A vast crowd gathered before the Winter Palace with a red flag emblazoned "Freedom of Assembly." In Moscow 50,000 people danced and sang the *Marseillaise,* the anthem of the French Revolution.

Meanwhile, Nicholas and Alexandra were struggling with a personal calamity of unimaginable proportions. In August 1904 Alexandra, after bearing four daughters, had at long last presented Nicholas with their life's desire, a son and heir. Tiny grand duke Alexei Nikolaevich was a splendid baby: chubby and pink,

with a head of curly blond hair and his mother's large blue-gray eyes. The two parents were beside themselves with joy. But then, when Alexei was six weeks old, Alexandra noticed in horror that her child was bleeding from the navel. Doctors eventually stemmed the flow. But their diagnosis was shattering: Alexei suffered from hemophilia, an incurable, virtually untreatable, largely fatal genetic flaw that prevented his blood from clotting properly. Moreover it was she, Alexandra, who had inflicted this hideous curse upon her cherished son.

Though helpless against it, medical science knew that the defective gene was transmitted only by females, primarily to their male offspring. There was no pattern of occurrence and no way of telling who might be a hemophilic carrier. In Alexandra's case, she had inherited the gene from her grandmother, Queen Victoria. Of Victoria's nine children, one of her four sons was a hemophiliac, and two of her five daughters, Princesses Alice and Beatrice, were hemophilic carriers. When the daughters of Alice and Beatrice married into the royal houses of Russia and Spain, their sons, the heirs to those two thrones, were born with hemophilia.

Little Alexei was an energetic boy, full of bounce and high spirits when life allowed him to be. But if he bruised himself, the bleeding would start beneath the skin and sometimes swell into a grapefruit-size hematoma before the pressure finally induced a clot. If the bleeding was in a joint, the agony would be extreme. He was bedridden for weeks at a time, Alexandra sitting by his side, listening to his moans of "Mama, help me, help me!" and kissing him on the hair, forehead, and eyes, as if the touch of her lips could somehow relieve his torment. "Think of the torture of that mother, an impotent witness of her son's martyrdom in those hours of anguish," recalled a friend, "a mother who knew that she herself was the cause of those sufferings."

Alexandra looked on Alexei's affliction as God's punishment for her sins. To atone, she donated money to churches, plunged into good works, and spent hour after hour lost in prayer. Be-

SNAPSHOTS OF A FAMILY

As tensions mounted in the empire, the royal family spent more and more time within the storybook confines of the Tsarskoe Selo estate. There in the beautiful countryside, Olga, Tatiana, Marie, Anastasia, and their little brother, Alexei, played under the watchful eyes of servants and nannies. Separated in age by less than 10 years, the children, seen at right in a 1904 family portrait, were each other's best friends, and while their personalities were different, they apparently functioned as a happy unit. Olga was known for her kindness and intellect, Tatiana for her elegance, Marie for her sunny disposition, and Anastasia—nicknamed Shvibzik, or "Imp"—for her mischievous wit.

The family also spent time together on spring and fall trips to the Crimea and summers on the Baltic coast or aboard the royal yacht *Standart.* During these relaxing times, Nicholas and Alexandra indulged their children's playfulness, even joining in themselves. When the children grew old enough, each was given a small box camera, and together with their parents they began to take pictures that were later pasted into scrapbooks and photo albums. A selection of these snapshots is shown on the following two pages, a photographic record of a loving family whose carefree days were destined soon to end.

With Anastasia in the saddle, two-year-old Alexei tugs at their pony's reins while his older sisters await their rides. Though often in pain, the tsarevich loved rough-and-tumble games, much to his parents' distress.

On a 1908 shore excursion in Finland, Tatiana, Marie, and Anastasia amuse themselves with a swing. The playful Anastasia grins for the camera.

A serious amateur photographer herself, Alexandra adjusts her camera during a 1910 cruise on the royal yacht *Standart.*

Alexei plays with a toy drum on the *Standart* in 1907. "How beautiful he was," remembered a family friend, "how healthy, how normal, with his golden hair, his shining blue eyes."

Having just returned from picking wildflowers, Anastasia, Tatiana, Marie, and Olga gather on a Baltic Sea beach in 1910. Anastasia holds a floral crown along with her camera.

Sixteen-year-old Olga *(front)*, 12-year-old Marie, and a lady-in-waiting enjoy the company of the *Standart*'s officers during a cruise on the Black Sea in 1911.

Anastasia practices her knitting in her mother's boudoir at Tsarskoe Selo. The four sisters were accomplished at needlework, drawing, and piano.

At left, Olga and Tatiana—the "big pair"—relax outside the Livadia Palace in the Crimea with their French tutor. The family was fluent in French, English, and German as well as Russian.

Shovel in hand, Nicholas strikes a conqueror's pose over the partly buried Alexei during a 1916 outing to a Dnieper River beach. The tsar delighted in the pranks and play of his children.

These unemployed workers share communal bowls of kasha, or buckwheat gruel, in a St. Petersburg soup kitchen. Dried sunflower seeds constituted the other principal staple of the poor. Meanwhile, at right, aristocratic guests dine sumptuously at Countess Elizabeth Shuvalova's Ball of the Colored Wigs. The chasm between social classes, already vast, widened greatly in the years before the First World War with the influx into the capital of peasants seeking factory work.

tween attacks, when she saw her son with rosy cheeks and listened to him laugh, she would exclaim, "God has heard me. He has pitied my sorrow at last." But then the disease would strike again, and the clouds of despair would blot out her sun.

At the tsar and tsarina's insistence, Alexei's condition was guarded like the deepest state secret. No one must know that the future emperor was an invalid living constantly in the shadow of death. The health of the imperial family was not a subject for public discussion in any case. But Nicholas and Alexandra carried their secrecy to such an extreme that it fueled every sort of rumor about the lad and, indeed, about the tsar and tsarina—most particularly after the appearance in November 1905 of a disreputable peasant wanderer known as Grigory Rasputin.

The man was in his mid-30s when he arrived from Siberia with a reputation as a

hypnotic preacher and faith healer. Under the sponsorship of the Orthodox Church, which was looking for such peasant holy men to revive its influence among the masses, Rasputin was introduced as a repentant sinner whom God had blessed with extraordinary powers of healing and clairvoyance. Smelling like a goat and acting like one, this strange creature made an instant hit with St. Petersburg's jaded, curiosity-seeking society and quickly came to the attention of the tsar and tsarina.

"We have got to know a man of God, Grigory," Nicholas told his diary. And to Alexandra, praying for a miracle to cure Alexei, Rasputin soon seemed like a gift from heaven itself. He prophesied that her son would not die, that the disease would disappear when Alexei reached 13; and in his hypnotic way, he did soothe the child, which in turn appeared to help the bleeding. To the devout Nicholas and Alexandra, what could be more natural than a man of God succeeding where all the doctors had failed? Rasputin's visits to the palace became more frequent as he quickly established a favored position with the Crown.

As a result of the October Manifesto, the tsar retained his essential powers, including a veto over Duma legislation and the right to dissolve the new legislative body altogether. Yet the

RED FLAG OF REVOLUTION

The revolutions sweeping Europe in 1848 that aimed to replace monarchical rule with representative government fell short of their lofty goals. They did, however, have an impact on their neighbors to the east. Inspired by the citizens at the barricades in Paris and Berlin, young radicals in Moscow and St. Petersburg were determined to bring constitutional and social change to autocratic Russia.

Until the 1880s, the radicals believed that revolution in overwhelmingly rural Russia would spring from an impoverished peasantry ready to rise against the landowners. But Russia's peasants distrusted the motives of the upper-class radicals, identifying them with the landowners, and possessed an almost mystical reverence for the tsar.

Some radicals turned to Marxism and began to shift their focus to the urban proletariat. The Bolshevik Party of Vladimir Lenin recruited members from this class and dramatized their revolutionary potential in paintings such as Boris Kustodiev's *The Bolshevik, 1905 (above)*. In the painting, Kustodiev portrays an idealized worker who is carrying the red flag of revolution through Moscow. Such flags had been held aloft by French revolutionaries as a symbol of liberty, republicanism, and social emancipation. In the future, the red flag would become as synonymous with the new Soviet state as the traditional symbols of bread and salt were with old Russia.

Duma enjoyed sufficient responsibilities to guarantee chaos if it chose to defy Nicholas and his ministers.

In the initial election, between 20 and 25 million adult male Russians went to the polls for the first time. They returned 497 deputies, including members of two dozen young parties, mostly of liberal to radical bent. More than 100 deputies were unaffiliated peasants; representation had been weighted heavily toward the countryside in hopes that the peasantry's traditional awe of the tsar would work in his favor.

But the Duma's mood was evident the moment the deputies filed into the throne room of the Winter Palace on May 10, 1906, to be received by Nicholas, his court, and his ministers. Dowager Empress Marie was startled by the "incomprehensible hatred" on the faces opposite, and the reform-minded Pyotr Stolypin, who had replaced Sergei Witte as prime minister, wondered if one particularly insolent fellow "might throw a bomb."

Immediately thereafter, the Duma formulated an address to the throne that began, "The greatest ulcer of our public life is the despotism of the government's officials," and went on to demand, among other things, the right to strike, elimination of all class privilege, abolition of the death penalty, redistribution of Crown and church lands, and amnesty for all those participating in the 1905 revolution. Elected for five years, the first Duma lasted just 73 days before Nicholas sent it packing.

The second Duma was worse. Now, the ultraradical Bolsheviks, Mensheviks, and socialist revolutionaries, who had boycotted the first elections, entered the lists, and their appearance galvanized the forces of the far right. The result was an extreme polarization that caused Nicholas to dismiss the second Duma after three months. "What you want are great upheavals," Prime Minister Stolypin boomed at his enemies on the left. "But what we want is a Great Russia."

Obviously Stolypin had to find himself a more tractable Duma if he hoped to achieve his major goal: land reform that would mean something to Russia's peasants. His answer was to manufacture one. In June 1907, at Stolypin's behest, Nicholas arbitrarily changed the electoral law to reduce worker and peasant representation in the Duma while dramatically increasing that of the gentry. Although not illegal, it was underhanded—and it was also effective. The next two Dumas lived out their terms in a spirit of cooperation, while the government got on with its legislative program.

The core of Stolypin's land reform was an end to the inefficient, initiative-robbing village commune and the establishment of a class of strong, independent, individual farmers whose success depended on stability. Under the communal system, which managed virtually all peasant-owned land, a peasant might be allocated as many as 50 scattered strips, each containing a few rows of corn or wheat, and he often spent as much time walking to and fro as he did cultivating the crop.

With the blessings of Nicholas and the new Duma, Stolypin decreed that any peasant who wished could withdraw from the commune and claim his share of land; the plot was to be in one piece, not fragments, and a family elder could bequeath it to one or all of his children as he chose. Further, the commune could be abolished altogether by a vote of the peasants. To help the program along, the imperial family sold four million acres of Crown lands to the government, which in turn made them available on easy terms to individual peasants.

As it happened, the noisiest peasant agitators were often the first to claim land and thus became supporters of law and order. The program prospered, until by 1914, nine million peasant families owned their farms. The pious Nicholas could see God's hand in it, too, for from 1906 to 1911, Russia enjoyed warm summers, mild winters, and all the gentle rain a farmer could wish. Crop yields exceeded anything in history. And with plentiful food, a prosperity of sorts arrived: Tax revenues rose; the government budget showed a surplus; foreign nations were encouraged to grant loans; the railway system expanded; iron and coal mines broke records for production.

In the Duma, the government passed bills raising teachers' salaries and promoting free primary-school education. Press censorship was relaxed and there were some gains in civil liberties and tolerance of minority religions.

Yet if Stolypin charted significant advances for the peasants and certain others, conditions in Russia's urban factories remained abominable, with long hours, low pay, and disgraceful conditions. Although wages increased by about one-fourth in the years following 1905, prices rose far more quickly—to the point where eight out of 10 workers in St. Petersburg earned less than the minimum survival wage that had been established by a government commission.

And matters grew worse as unsuccessful peasant farmers displaced by Stolypin's agrarian reform poured into the cities in search of jobs. Between 1910 and 1914, the ranks of the urban proletariat swelled by 600,000 workers, most of them young and angry, with no chastening memory of defeat in 1905. They began to radicalize the cities anew; in 1911, perhaps 100,000 workers had gone on strike at one time or another; the next year, the number climbed sevenfold; and by 1914, one out of every two Russian workers had taken part in a labor dispute during the preceding 12 months.

Whether Pyotr Stolypin could have defused this explosive situation became moot on the evening of September 14, 1911. Accompanying the tsar to Kiev, Stolypin was attending a performance at the opera when a young man in evening dress walked up and fired two bullets into his chest. Stolypin died four days later. His assassin was identified as a leftist double agent, a revolutionary pretending to be an informer; that was how he had acquired a police ticket to the opera. But suspicions lingered that the murder was actually the work of ultrarightists connected to the police. Both extremes had ample reason to detest Stolypin.

His hypnotic eyes leveled at the camera, Grigory Rasputin picks at his unkempt beard. With his long, greasy hair, teeth black from neglect, and fingernails encrusted with dirt, the self-proclaimed holy man was as well known for his slovenly habits as for his prowess as a healer.

His successors lacked Stolypin's strength and vision. Russia would continue along her erratic course of agrarian reform and smoldering urban revolt until she was engulfed by world war.

March 6, 1913, should have been one of the glorious days in Russian history, the day selected to mark 300 years of Romanov rule. Artillery boomed in salute; memorial Masses were chanted and congratulatory manifestos proclaimed. Yet it was a joyless tricentennial for the residents of St. Petersburg and their monarchs.

Never outgoing, Nicholas of late had withdrawn even further into the seclusion of Tsarskoe Selo. In his few public appearances he wore a somber visage, his manner detached and remote, and on this occasion he offered little reason for national rejoicing.

fan of white eagle feathers in her hand trembled; her face became flushed, her breathing labored. "Presently," wrote the ambassador's daughter, "it seemed that this emotion or distress mastered her completely, and with a few whispered words to the Emperor she rose and withdrew to the back of the box, to be no more seen that evening." Nor did she appear again in public for many weeks.

St. Petersburg society took this for an affront, yet a further example of the cold aloofness they had come to expect from their empress. Naturally shy, upset by the tragic circumstances attending her marriage and coronation, she could never force herself to campaign for the hearts of her court lords and ladies. Over time, a mutual antipathy had arisen, and the tricentennial had reinforced it. That aside, in the winter of 1913, there was still another reason

"The lamps are going out all over Europe. We shall not see them lit again in our lifetime."

The crowds at the ceremonies remained strangely silent.

His tsarina, Alexandra, might have been in another world. The hemophilia of eight-year-old Alexei had not relaxed its grip. And Alexandra, her health and spirits afflicted by grief over her son, ever more dependent on Rasputin for comfort and hope, had become a near-invalid herself, reclusive, often taking to her bed, prone to bouts of hysteria that Nicholas was helpless to assuage.

At a celebratory opera performance, Alexandra appeared in the imperial box for the first time in years. "Her lovely, tragic face was expressionless, almost austere, as she stood by her husband's side during the playing of the National Anthem," recalled the daughter of the British ambassador. No smile acknowledged the applause that greeted the anthem's conclusion, and a growing travail came over Alexandra as the performance wore on. The

to dislike her: Her origins were German, and to Russians everything Teutonic was increasingly offensive.

Over the past half-dozen years, political and military tensions had been escalating among the Great Powers—between Russia and her allies France and Britain on one side and the Central Powers of Austria-Hungary and Germany on the other. Now, as matters grew worse, there was the empress Alexandra, once again that "German woman."

The flash point came on June 28, 1914, when Archduke Francis Ferdinand, heir to the Austro-Hungarian throne, was assassinated during a state visit to the Serbian city of Sarajevo. While the Serbian government had played no role in the plot, the outraged Austrians issued an insulting, 48-hour ultimatum that no nation with a shred of honor could accept. When the Serbs re-

This poster soliciting "Aid for the Victims of War" appeared shortly after the outbreak of hostilities with Germany in August 1914. "Crowds stood before the poster and old women wept," recalled the artist Leonid Pasternak, father of writer Boris Pasternak.

jected the demands, in as conciliatory terms as possible, the Austrians declared war and at 5:00 a.m. on July 29 started lobbing shells across the Danube into the Serbian capital of Belgrade.

Russia had long seen itself as the champion of Serbia and, indeed, all Slavic peoples. But in St. Petersburg, Nicholas dithered, praying for peace, not comprehending the avalanche hurtling down on him. Though he declared his support of the Serbs, he would permit only partial mobilization against the Austrians—thus leaving naked Russia's long border facing a supremely well-armed German army. With the imperial general staff wringing its hands, Nicholas agreed to an audience with Foreign Minister Sergei Sazonov at 3:00 p.m. on July 30. Sazonov spoke with his tsar for an hour. Nicholas asked, "You think that it is too late to save the peace?" Sazonov replied that it was. Nicholas went pale and seemed to have difficulty speaking. "Just think of the responsibility you are advising me to assume," he said, and then, a bit later, "You are right. There is nothing left for us to do. . . . Give my order for mobilization to the Chief of the General Staff."

On August 1 Germany declared war against Russia and later against France and Britain. Austria did the same. "The lamps are going out all over Europe," said Sir Edward Grey, the British foreign minister who had negotiated the Anglo-Russian alliance back in 1907. "We shall not see them lit again in our lifetime."

As in the first days of the Japanese war, waves of patriotism swept over Russia. On the afternoon of August 2, Nicholas and Alexandra entered the Winter Palace's immense Salle de Nicholas, where 5,000 people waited, men and women frantically trying to kiss the tsar's hand as he passed. An altar had been set up, and upon it stood the miraculous Virgin of Kazan, the icon before which the grizzled Kutuzov had prayed before leading Russia's armies against Napoleon. Nicholas solemnly invoked the icon, raising his right arm and pronouncing the oath taken by Alexander I in 1812: "I solemnly swear that I will never make peace so long as a single enemy remains on Russian soil."

In the enormous square outside, thousands fell to their knees singing the imperial anthem when Nicholas and Alexandra appeared on a balcony high above them. "Batyushka! Batyushka!" they chanted. "Lead us to victory! God save the Tsar!" "At that moment," mused an observer, "the Tsar was really the Autocrat, the military, political, and religious director of his people, the absolute master of their bodies and souls."

In cities and towns throughout the empire, strikes ceased as if by magic. Workers threw down the red flags of revolution to hold up portraits of Nicholas. "For faith, Tsar, and country! For the defense of Holy Russia!" echoed through factories and villages, barracks and universities. Aristocrat and commoner alike felt the stirrings. "This is not a political war," advised a grand duchess. "It is a duel to the death between Slavism and Germanism." An elderly peasant was of the same mind. "If we are unlucky enough not to destroy the Germans," he told a noble, "they'll come here. Then they'll harness you and me—yes, you as well as me—to their plows."

In St. Petersburg, mobs ransacked the German embassy. Reactionaries and ultraliberals in the Duma clasped hands, while the government immediately changed the capital's westernized name to the unquestionably Russian Petrograd. "I now look on the future with complete confidence," said Nicholas, as sturdy youths in every corner of his empire shouldered their packs and jammed into cattle cars headed for the front.

The confidence would not last. Launching an advance into East Prussia from Russian-ruled Poland, the tsar's armies suffered the bloodiest carnage the world had yet seen. From August 1914 to August 1915, Russia lost half of its army: 1,400,000 men killed and another 976,000 taken prisoner. Russian generals sent cavalry riding at German artillery, and the cream of aristocratic Russian youth died in their saddles. Waves of foot soldiers charged into German lines bristling with machine guns and massed rifles. The regiments just melted into the ground.

A tide of ragged, starving refugees flooded the cities, washing away the last vestiges of optimism, unity, and national reconciliation. Angry mobs roamed the streets demanding more food, lower prices, higher pay, and the freedoms and reforms so long denied them. Hatred of the Jews, never far from the surface, led to looting, beatings, and murder. New venom was directed at Alexandra for her German heritage.

In these days of defeat and unrest, Nicholas was beside himself with anxiety. Finally, he decided to act. At a meeting of the council of ministers in late August 1915, the war minister informed his colleagues, "This morning His Majesty told me of his decision to personally assume the supreme command of the army."

The ministers were aghast. Their sovereign was about to abandon state responsibilities for a military headquarters 500 miles away. Yet the more they pleaded, the more stubborn Nicholas became. Mystically convinced of his God-given mission, of his oneness with "the people," he had always hated to let the war unfold at a distance. It was a tsar's divine duty to lead his armies in battle. And so he went to preside at the front—leaving Russia's internal affairs largely in the hands of his wife and empress.

The war had worked a dramatic change in Alexandra. Far from being a German sympathizer, she was after 20 years an ardent Russian patriot. She still agonized over Alexei's hemophilia, and her own health remained fragile enough to require a wheelchair at times in the privacy of the palace. Yet fresh energy and purpose welled up within her. She began to train as a nurse and spent mornings in the operating room, afternoons visiting the 85 hospitals under her patronage in and around Petrograd alone. Dying men reached out to touch her as she knelt to pray beside their cots.

Alexandra also sought to inspire Nicholas. She constantly urged—almost commanded—him to be more forceful: It must be his war, his peace, his honor. "Forgive me precious one, but you know you are too kind and gentle—sometimes a good loud voice can do wonders," she wrote him. "How I wish I could pour

Mutinous soldiers aboard a commandeered government car openly display a red flag in Petrograd on February 27, 1917. Previously, the vehicle, a Rolls-Royce, had been used to provide shore transportation for the officers of the royal yacht *Standart*.

my will into your veins . . . Be Peter the Great, Ivan the Terrible . . . Crush them all under you."

Small wonder that the man who would one day soon describe himself, only half-jokingly, as "your poor little weak-willed hubby" felt a desperate need for Alexandra upon leaving Petrograd. "Think, my wifey," he wrote, shortly after reaching army headquarters, "will you not come to the assistance of your hubby now that he is absent?" And in a letter the next day he wrote, "You will really help me by speaking to the ministers and watching them."

Alexandra would take him at his word. And continually at her side, his prayers "arising day and night," as she put it, would be Grigory Rasputin.

In the decade since his arrival, Rasputin had forged an unassailable bond with the imperial family. Time and again, through some unknown power, he stemmed Alexei's bleeding—and what made it more awesome still was that he did not even have to be present. On one occasion, in October 1912, the eight-year-old tsarevich had been so near death that a priest administered the last rites. Rasputin happened to be visiting his hometown in Siberia and could be reached only by telegram. He responded, "God has seen your tears and heard your prayers. Do not grieve. The little one will not die." Within hours, a miraculous recovery commenced.

To Alexandra—and, through her, to Nicholas as well—"our friend" could do no wrong. But everyone else had come to know him as a vile charlatan, an obscene drunk and lecher, who used his enormous influence to extort whatever he wished from men and women of every age and station. Stories buzzed that he had made the tsar wash his filthy feet; that he was bedding Alexandra; that he had raped all the daughters and turned them into harem concubines. It was nonsense, of course, but Rasputin did nothing to stop the gossip. Rather, he encouraged it, bragging that he had exposed himself to the tsar and could do what he liked with "the old girl."

The stories reached the palace, but were given no credence. Rasputin was a man of God, his credentials proved by his healing prayers. When Nicholas went off to the war, Alexandra drew ever closer to Rasputin as her confidant, adviser, and yardstick in dealing with the government's ministers. A "good man" was someone who had good things to say about Rasputin; a "bad man" hated Rasputin and made up disgusting stories about him. Alexandra herself had often irrational but unshakable opinions about people, and when she discovered that she rather liked the role of autocrat, at times comparing herself to Catherine the Great, she did not hesitate to have her husband sack anyone who displeased her. "I am your wall in the rear," she wrote Nicholas. "Don't laugh at silly old wifey, but she has trousers on unseen."

By the end of 1916, some sort of change at the top seemed inevitable. The mildest of the conspirators hoped to exile Alexandra to her palace in the Crimea for the duration of the war; others considered a palace coup to depose the tsar himself. Of them all,

Bolshevik demonstrators on Nevsky Prospect, Petrograd's main street, scatter after coming under machine-gun fire from troops loyal to the provisional government. Continued unrest throughout the summer would lead to full-scale revolution in the fall and the subsequent Bolshevik takeover of the country.

the only plot that succeeded was the one to murder Rasputin.

On December 29, three nobles of the court, led by Prince Felix Yusupov, along with a right-wing deputy from the Duma, invited Rasputin to a late-evening soiree at Yusupov's palace in Petrograd. Monarchists to the core, Yusupov and the others detested Rasputin for his evil influence over the tsar; by killing him they would cleanse the throne and restore the dynasty's prestige.

On the fatal day, Rasputin was warned not to visit Yusupov by an acquaintance who sensed a plot. Rasputin himself seemed apprehensive and spent much time in prayer. But the conspirators knew their man's tastes. Yusupov had recently married an exquisite woman, one of Petrograd's reigning beauties; she would be present, Rasputin was told, and he lusted after her.

While Rasputin awaited the lady, the conspirators plied him with several glasses of poisoned Madeira wine along with a number of cyanide-laced cakes. An hour passed. Nothing. The poison had no apparent effect. In exasperation, Yusupov hauled out a revolver and shot him in the side. Rasputin toppled to the floor with a wild scream, then lay silent as the assassins went off to dump his overcoat before disposing of the body in the Neva River. But their victim was a tough bird. Rasputin regained consciousness and lurched out into the courtyard shrieking, "Felix! Felix! I will tell the Tsarina everything!"

Two more bullets put him down again. And with a heavy kick on the temple for good measure, the assassins weighted Grigory Rasputin with chains, drove to a remote spot, and dumped him into the Neva. When his body washed up two days later, an autopsy revealed that he had died of drowning.

The death of Rasputin brought Nicholas ever closer to his wife. Alexandra was disconsolate at first, anguished over the loss of her holy man and what might now happen to Alexei. But after a few days, her tears and hysterics gave way to a steely resolve to maintain the autocracy bestowed on Russia by God, to

rule with her husband—or if he did not show enough spine, perhaps even to act for him.

But nothing changed; and nothing would change. The revolution began in March.

The immediate cause was food. In the most severe winter in years, the urban masses of northern and central Russia were perilously close to starvation. Caloric intakes fell by a quarter, infant mortality doubled, crime rates tripled, and children were sent into the streets as prostitutes. "What has happened to Civilization!" agonized the writer Maxim Gorky, after one such encounter. "On your way somewhere at night you see them shuffling along the sidewalks, just like cockroaches, blue with cold and hungry. . . . I talked to one of them. I put some money into her hand and hurried away, in tears."

From the autumn of 1915 on, long queues formed outside the bakeries, groceries, and butcher shops. After 10-hour shifts in the factories, women brought stools and benches on which to rest while waiting to buy tiny allotments. The queues became a sort of forum, where information and views were exchanged, and where the grumbling turned to bitter anger, and the anger grew into a terrible, swelling rage.

On Thursday, March 8, 1917, a group of female textile workers in the Petrograd bread lines lost all endurance. When they were told that there was no bread available, they broke into the bakeries to help themselves. Then they went to get their menfolk in nearby factories, intending a protest march to the center of the city. By the thousands, the men and women streamed across the Neva bridges chanting, "Give us bread! Give us bread!" Troops of mounted Cossacks waving whips dispersed the mob, but the people were back the next morning, their numbers multiplying.

On Saturday, March 10, Petrograd came to a standstill as virtually every worker took to the streets, carrying red banners and shouting, "Down with the war!" "Down with the German woman!" For the first time, serious alarm jolted the government;

cabinet ministers met throughout the day, desperately and hopelessly trying to solve the food shortages. They wired Nicholas at army headquarters imploring him to return. But the tsar, believing that the crisis was just another rash of strikes, only wired back: "I order that the disorders . . . be ended tomorrow."

That meant force. The minister of internal affairs, a loathsome favorite of Alexandra's named Alexander Protopopov, made plans to meet the protesters with police, then with Cossacks, and finally with troops and machine-gun fire. The first shots were fired on Sunday, and before the day was out, 200 people had been killed; no one counted the wounded.

The shooting only energized the mobs—now in full revolt—and began to sicken the soldiers. Units met in their barracks, arguing, deciding. How could Russians slaughter Russians? At six o'clock on Monday morning, a sergeant in the famed Volinsky regiment shot his captain; the other officers fled, and the Volinsky marched out, band blaring, to join the revolution. The mutiny spread swiftly to other celebrated regiments—the Semonovsky, the Ismailovsky, the Litovsky, finally the Preobrazhensky Guard, the oldest regiment in the army, created by Peter the Great himself.

In Petrograd that day, soldiers and workers set ablaze the law courts, the ministry of internal affairs, the headquarters of the secret police, and a score of police stations across the city. They burst open the gates of the arsenal and emptied the prisons. Looters roamed the streets at will. Maxim Gorky watched the Palace of Justice go up in flames. "A tall stooping man in a shaggy sheepskin hat was walking about like a sentinel," he wrote. "He stopped and asked in a dull voice: Well, it means that all justice is to be abolished, doesn't it? Punishments all done away with, is that it? No one answered him."

The president of the legislative Duma, the loyal and able Mikhail Rodzianko, wired telegram after telegram to Nicholas describing the anarchy and pleading with his tsar to form a min-

Watched by armed guards, Nicholas sits dejectedly on a tree stump at Tsarskoe Selo shortly after his abdication. In August 1917 the tsar and his family were transferred to Siberia, where, less than a year later, they were executed by a Bolshevik firing squad.

istry that would command the people's confidence. Nicholas had ignored him at first, saying, "That fat Rodzianko has sent me some nonsense which I shall not even bother to answer." Only late Monday night, when a terse telegram arrived from Alexandra, did he begin to grasp the truth. The empress who had recently said, "There is no revolution in Russia, nor could there be. God would not allow it," now wired: "Concessions inevitable. Street fighting continues. Many units gone over to the enemy. Alix."

Nicholas ordered his train made ready and at 5:00 a.m. Tuesday started off for Petrograd. Even then, he had avoided the question of a new government, saying that he would decide when he reached his palace at Tsarskoe Selo. It was far too late in any case. Power had already passed from the tsar's government to the Duma. Around midday, with no hope of action by Nicholas, the imperial cabinet had dissolved itself, and the ministers had placed

their persons under the protection of the Duma, where a provisional government was forming. Those who wished to save the throne were agreed on one thing: Nicholas must not be overthrown by force; he must abdicate.

The tsar learned of these developments on the morning of Thursday, March 15, soon after his train reached Pskov, 150 miles from Petrograd. Rodzianko had taken the precaution of consulting Russia's military chiefs, and the answering telegrams were laid before the tsar. All were in accord: He had to go. Nicholas was staggered. The blood drained from his face. He turned to a window, lifted the shade, and peered out. No one would know precisely what passed through his mind at that moment. But

civil war, a counterrevolution with his beloved Russia in flames, with his people killing each other—that would not have been an option for this gentle man.

Nicholas turned from the window and announced in a strong, clear voice, "I have decided that I shall give up the throne in favor of my son, Alexei." He made the sign of the cross, and the others in the car crossed themselves also. Then Tsar Nicholas II went home to Tsarskoe Selo and his Alexandra, on whose bosom he laid his head and cried his heart out.

On reflection, Nicholas realized that his hemophilic son was not physically fit to be tsar, and instead chose as his successor his brother Mikhail, who promptly declined. The dynasty of the Romanovs was over. But the downfall of autocracy and the establishment of a provisional government failed to stem the economic and

"There is no revolution in Russia, nor could there be. God would not allow it."

political turmoil that had been steadily growing since the early months of the war. Revolution simmered throughout the summer, then flamed anew the following November.

The victors this time would be the Bolshevik revolutionaries led by Vladimir Ilyich Lenin, who had spent his adult life preparing for this moment. But, the Bolshevik takeover in the winter of 1917, brutal and vindictive, unpalatable to vast numbers of Russians, would itself spawn further violence. Russia, already so bloodied, would suffer through several years of civil war before the Bolsheviks eventually prevailed and the Soviet state, as ruthless and repressive as its autocratic predecessor, came clanking into being.

A REBIRTH OF RUSSIAN CULTURE

The rulers of 18th-century Russia were so successful in introducing European customs and ideas to their subjects that, for the aristocracy, Russian culture almost ceased to exist. Nobles spoke, read, and wrote in French, and they hired English, German, or French tutors for their children. With the dawning of the 19th century, however, came a renewed interest in things uniquely Russian, and a rebirth of Russian culture that is generally attributed to one man, writer Alexander Sergeyevich Pushkin.

Pushkin, shown here in an 1827 portrait by the serf artist Orest Kiprensky, is credited with laying the foundation for a national literature written in Russian, based on Russian traditions, and full of the exuberance of Russian life. Born in 1799 to an aristocrat and his wife, who counted among her forebears an Abyssinian prince, Pushkin was schooled by foreign tutors and cared for by a peasant nurse.

It was this nurse, Anna Rodionovna, who recited to him the magical folk and fairy tales of the Russian people and instilled in him a love of the Russian language.

During his short career —he died in a duel at age 37—Pushkin produced epic dramas such as *Boris Godunov*, which told the story of a 16th-century pretender to the Russian throne; short stories; poetry; lyric songs; and his famous novel in verse, *Eugene Onegin*. All shared an elegant and mellifluous style, drew on observations of everyday life, and dealt with major themes that persist in Russian literature today.

Pushkin influenced his contemporaries as well as later composers, authors, and artists. The novels of Tolstoy and Dostoyevsky, the ballets of Tchaikovsky, the music of Mussorgsky, the paintings of Ilya Repin, and the theater of Chekhov and Stanislavsky owe much to the uniquely Russian voice of Alexander Pushkin.

By the time artist Ivan Kramskoi completed this portrait of the middle-aged Leo Tolstoy, the author had married and penned his epic novel, *War and Peace*. A veteran of the Crimean War, Tolstoy called upon his experiences from that conflict when crafting the book's vivid battle scenes.

Tolstoy and his wife, Sofia *(seated at center, on either side of the samovar)*, dine outdoors with family and friends at their country estate, Yasnaya Polyana.

A GOLDEN AGE OF RUSSIAN LITERATURE

Alexander Pushkin is said to have ushered in the golden age of Russian literature, and indeed, within two generations, Russia had produced the greatest masters of prose fiction the world had ever known. In 1840 Mikhail Lermontov, who inherited Pushkin's mantle as Russia's national poet after the death of his friend, wrote the acclaimed novel *A Hero of Our Time*.

And in 1842 the self-effacing Nikolai Gogol, also Pushkin's friend, completed a searing parody of Russia's system of serfdom entitled *Dead Souls*.

Ivan Turgenev, an aristocrat who wrote empathetically about the serfs, published *A Sportsman's Sketches* in 1852. This book so shocked Russia with its revealing descriptions of the daily agonies of rural

peasant life that Turgenev was arrested and confined to his estate for 18 months for "propagating opinions detrimental to the respect due to the nobility from other classes." Later it was said that his book figured in the 1861 decision by Alexander II to abolish serfdom.

By the mid-19th century, the writers Feodor Dostoyevsky and Leo Tolstoy were

Writer Feodor Dostoyevsky, shown in an 1872 portrait by Vasily Perov, attempted to portray "the depths of the human soul." The manuscript page at left is from *The Possessed,* about a terrorist's murder by his co-conspirators in a plot to assassinate Tsar Alexander II.

using the novel as a prism through which to examine and debate many social and spiritual issues of the time. A dark and brooding personality, Dostoyevsky suffered from epilepsy, compulsive gambling, and wretched poverty. His novels, such as *Crime and Punishment* and *The Brothers Karamazov,* explored the dark impulses of humankind and showed read-

ers the underbelly of Russian life—from slums to prisons to Siberian wastelands. He searched for meaning in every aspect of the human experience.

Tolstoy, an aristocrat by birth, chose the epic canvas of Russia's defeat of Napoleon for his masterpiece, *War and Peace,* widely considered to be the greatest of all Russian novels. He came to re-

gard peasants as Russia's heroes, and in *War and Peace* allowed the true meaning of life to be revealed only to a peasant. The crowning achievement of these two authors was the creation of a national literature that laid the compelling questions of human freedom, divine justice, and the eternal struggle between good and evil before Russia and the world.

Peter Ilyich Tchaikovsky, shown here in a 19th-century painting, reconciled his classical European musical training with his Russian patriotism: The composer based many of his most beautiful symphonies, operas, and ballets on Russian history and folk myths, as well as on the works of Alexander Pushkin.

Russian bass Feodor Chaliapin *(standing behind the pianist)* entertains a gathering at the home of music critic Vladimir Stasov *(seated at center).*

A SMALL BUT MIGHTY HANDFUL

Music in Russia was not immune to the wave of nationalism that was sweeping the country. During the 19th century, a growing circle of energetic young Russians dedicated themselves to writing symphonies, songs, and operas based on the poems of Pushkin, the dance melodies of gypsies, the songs of riverboatmen, and the age-old chants of the Russian liturgy.

Mikhail Glinka was the first of this emerging group of composers to marry European musical form with Russian themes. His first opera, *A Life for the Tsar,* written in 1836, was wildly popular with audiences. After Glinka, Russian musicians split into two camps—the Slavophiles, who revered everything Russian, reviled everything European, and eschewed formal mu-

sical training; and the so-called Westernizers, who preferred music that was Slavic in feel but European in form.

From the Slavophiles there emerged "a small but mighty handful," in the words of critic Vladimir Stasov, of young musicians and composers. The group, headed by musician and conductor Mily Balakirev, counted among its members physician and

Composer Modest Mussorgsky, here in a portrait by artist Ilya Repin, created many of Russia's most brilliant musical works, including the gripping *Night on Bald Mountain*. He also set to music Pushkin's drama *Boris Godunov;* the title page of the first edition of the score appears below.

БОРИСЪ ГОДУНОВЪ

опера въ 4^{хъ} ДѢЙСТВІЯХЪ съ прологомъ
СОЧИНЕНІЕ

М. П. МУСОРГСКАГО.

ПОЛНОЕ ПЕРЕЛОЖЕНІЕ (СО ВКЛЮЧЕНІЕМЪ СЦЕНЪ НЕ
ПРЕДПОЛАГАЕМЫХЪ КЪ ПОСТАНОВКѢ НА СЦЕНѢ) ДЛЯ
ФОРТЕПІЯНО СЪ ПѢНІЕМЪ.

Цѣна 10 р.с.

Собственность издателей для всѣхъ странъ.

ВАСИЛІЙ БЕССЕЛЬ и К^о

С. ПЕТЕРБУРГЪ.   МОСКВА.
Невскій проспектъ 54   Петровка д. Матвѣевой

research chemist Alexander Borodin, naval officer Nikolai Rimsky-Korsakov, military engineer César Cui, and a young officer of the Preobrazhensky Guard by the name of Modest Mussorgsky. Like Alexander Pushkin, Mussorgsky had grown up listening to colorful folk tales lovingly told by his peasant nanny. As an adult, he, along with the rest of this impassioned group,

was determined to create symphonic and operatic music that was truly Russian in both form and content.

The Westernizers blended a classical approach with Russian songs, stories, and settings. For a number of years, Peter Ilyich Tchaikovsky studied and taught at Russia's conservatories, absorbing European technique and style. But he also felt the attrac-

tion of Russian folk melodies. "I passionately love Russians," he once wrote, "the Russian language, the Russian mind, the Russian style of beauty, and Russian customs. I am a Russian in the fullest sense of the word." This sentiment is reflected in Tchaikovsky's masterpieces, which, though grounded in European technical expertise, seem to embody the Russian soul.

127

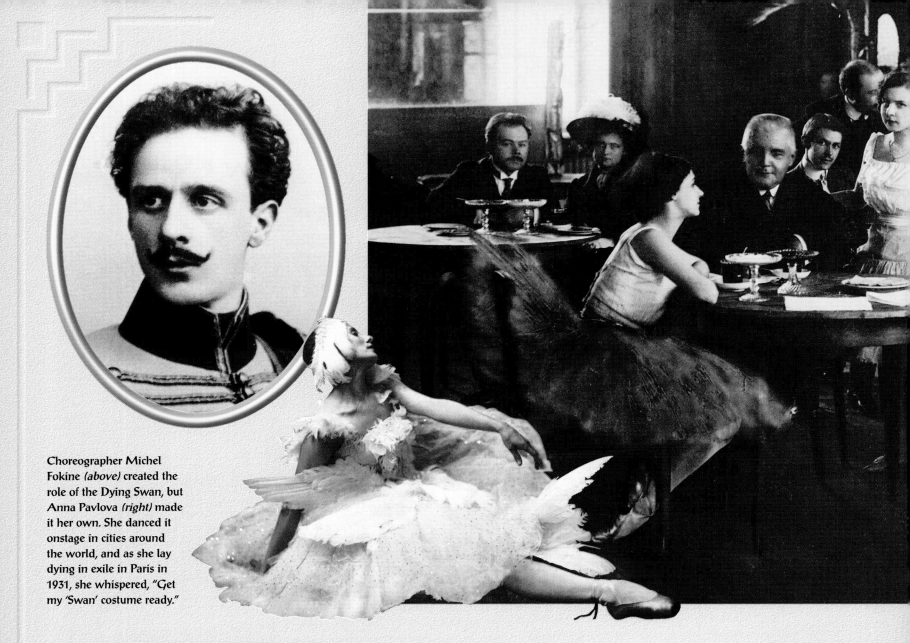

Choreographer Michel Fokine *(above)* created the role of the Dying Swan, but Anna Pavlova *(right)* made it her own. She danced it onstage in cities around the world, and as she lay dying in exile in Paris in 1931, she whispered, "Get my 'Swan' costume ready."

A PASSION FOR DANCE

From the time ballet first came to Russia from Europe during the 18th century, the Russian people embraced it with a singular passion. Ballet held great appeal to the Slavs and their traditional love of dance, and the marriage of fluid movement with music, colorful costumes, and sweeping drama was uniquely suited to bringing Russia's romantic legends and folk tales to the stage.

Although the Imperial School of Ballet opened in St. Petersburg in 1738, it was not until the 19th century that Russian ballet came into its own. In 1801 French dancer and choreographer Charles Didelot became the first choreographer to stage ballets with dramatic content—based on Pushkin's poetry—and raised Russian ballet to a level on a par with the best in Europe.

Next came the arrival of Marius Petipa, who presided over the Russian ballet for four decades and is considered to be the father of classical ballet. A Frenchman born into a ballet family, Petipa came to St. Petersburg as a dancer in 1857, was named ballet master of the Mariinsky Theater in 1862, and choreographed many original ballets. Petipa and Tchaikovsky

Dancers of the Ballets Russes dine after a St. Petersburg performance in 1909. Vaslav Nijinsky, who awed audiences with his effortless leaps, stands at extreme far right.

Sergei Diaghilev *(above)* developed artists of extraordinary talent for his Ballets Russes. After Pavlova turned down the title role in *The Firebird* because of its "horrible music," the part was danced by another of his prima ballerinas, Tamara Platonovna Karsavina *(left)*. Choreographed by Fokine and scored by Igor Stravinsky, *The Firebird* premiered in Paris to great acclaim in 1910.

enjoyed a fruitful collaboration, working together to match Petipa's stunning choreography with the great composer's soaring scores for *Swan Lake, The Nutcracker,* and *The Sleeping Beauty.*

Around the turn of the century, a young impresario of genius named Sergei Diaghilev decided to bring the spectacle of Russian ballet to the world. For his company, the Ballets Russes, Diaghilev encouraged a shift to the more natural and expressive style embraced by avant-garde Russian choreographer Michel Fokine. A new crop of superior dancers, including Anna Pavlova and Vaslav Nijinsky, were poised to take advantage of the new style. Far ahead of his time in his artistic concepts, Nijinsky shocked Paris with his scantily clad and erotic performance in Claude Debussy's *Afternoon of a Faun* and with his choreographic interpretation of Igor Stravinsky's *Rite of Spring.* Although Diaghilev decided in 1912 to move his ballet to Monte Carlo, his effect on Russian dance—and the effect of his dancers on the national consciousness—was profound and long lasting.

A YEARNING FOR REALISM

In 1863 the Russian Imperial Academy of Fine Arts was scandalized when more than a dozen of its best students, led by instructor Ivan Kramskoi, quit the academy to protest the composition theme imposed on them by their teachers. The chosen theme of "Odin at the Gates of Valhalla" for the academy's annual Gold Medal contest had no relevance for Russian artists in their struggle to uplift the Russian nation, the students asserted.

Leaving the prestige of the academy behind, the students, most of whom had humble origins, dedicated themselves to producing art based on a realistic portrayal of everyday life and formed an artists' cooperative to market their own works. Later, in 1871, the members, together with other artists of like mind, established themselves as the Society for Traveling Art Exhibitions, popularly known as *Peredvizhniki,* or the Wanderers. The society's artistic platform was "nationalism, populism, and realism," and Wanderers such as Nikolai Ge, Ilya Repin, Vasily Surikov, and Vasily Perov succeeded in producing paintings that reflected that doctrine.

Novelist Feodor Dostoyevsky hailed Ilya Repin's *Volga Barge Haulers* as an epic portrayal of the Russian people, praising the artist for disdaining simplistic themes of class struggle.

A 1901 portrait by Ilya Repin depicts St. Petersburg merchant and art benefactor Pavel Tretyakov in his gallery. Tretyakov spent a large part of his fortune to commission, purchase, and exhibit the work of Russian painters.

Repin's *Volga Barge Haulers,* considered the greatest Russian painting of the 19th century, exemplifies the work of the society's artists. Wishing to portray his subjects as individuals and not as downtrodden stereotypes, Repin spent months in the riverside villages where barge haulers plied their trade, doing pencil studies of them as they went about their work. The monu-mental finished painting depicts working men of all ages and stations.

Members of the society also vigorously pursued the goal of taking their art to the people. With the financial backing of merchant Pavel Tretyakov, the Wanderers sponsored hundreds of exhibitions in many parts of the country. Tretyakov, an avid collector of Russian art, eventually built a gallery to exhibit his collection and, in 1892, he gave the gallery to the city of Moscow. Today it houses many of Russia's greatest paintings, from the priceless 12th-century Byzantine icon *The Virgin of Vladimir* to the work of Valentin Serov, whose impressionist portraits provide a unique view of Russian high society as the age of imperial Russia came to an end.

Father of Method acting Konstantin Stanislavsky, shown here in a 1908 portrait by Valentin Serov, encouraged his actors to identify with their characters. To prepare for a production of Shakespeare's *Julius Caesar,* for example, he had them wear Roman togas around Moscow for days.

This scene from *Uncle Vanya* by Anton Chekhov shows the natural setting, realistic stage props, and period costumes favored by the Moscow Art Theater.

THEATER: INTO THE NEW CENTURY

Modern Russian theater was born in June 1897 during an 18-hour discussion between actor and director Konstantin Stanislavsky and playwright Vladimir Nemirovich-Danchenko that took place in Moscow's Bazaar restaurant. The two men felt constrained by the rules that held sway in Russian stagecraft: stilted, prescribed gestures for every emotion, such as a hand over the heart to denote great pain; furniture aligned in rigid patterns onstage regardless of the action; and severe limitations on costume design. Willing to stake their reputations on a new theater of realism, Stanislavsky and Nemirovich-Danchenko began to gather around them a group of talented young performers and writers who could help them realize their ideas.

The fledgling theater group approached merchants, industrialists, and wealthy patrons of the arts for financial support. One member of that circle was Savva Mamontov, owner of the Moscow Opera House. Since his theater had challenged the conventions of the imperial ballet and opera by utilizing modern scenery and staging, Stanislavksy and Nemirovich-Danchenko

The Moscow Art Theater staged the modern dramas of playwrights such as Anton Chekhov *(below, left)* and Maxim Gorky *(below, right)*. Chekhov's *The Seagull* had failed in St. Petersburg but drew large crowds in Moscow under Stanislavsky's direction. Its success ensured the survival of the theater, and in 1901 the company adopted the sea gull *(right)* as its emblem.

rightly believed he would be sympathetic to their cause.

The two entrepreneurs called their company the Moscow Art Theater and shared the responsibility of running it: Stanislavsky directed and acted, while Nemirovich-Danchenko scouted out new plays and supervised production. In the theater's first season, they swept away the stultifying conventions of traditional Russian theater, employing lifelike backdrops, natural movement, and realistic period dress.

Socialist organizer and playwright Maxim Gorky, Scandinavian playwright Henrik Ibsen, and actress Olga Knipper were among the artists raised to international prominence by the Moscow Art Theater. The theater's preeminent contributor, however, was playwright and novelist Anton Chekhov, son of a grocer and grandson of a Russian peasant, whose dramas embodied the "theater of inner feeling" nurtured by Stanislavsky. Chekhov, who died from tuberculosis at age 44, was eulogized by Tolstoy as "an artist of life. He is understood and accepted not only by every Russian, but by all humanity."

GLOSSARY

Abdicate: to formally relinquish the throne and the responsibilities inherent in it.

Adz: an axlike tool with a curved steel blade positioned on a wooden handle at a right angle, used for shaping wood.

Agronomist: one who studies or manages soil and field crops.

Alkonost: in Russian legend, a bird of sorrow; a fantastic creature, half bird, half woman, who could protect or destroy any man that fell under the spell of its beauty and song.

Amnesty: an act of forgiveness for past offenses; often granted by a government to an individual or a class of people.

Apothecary: one who prepares and sells drugs or compounds for medicinal purposes.

Aquiline: to be shaped like an eagle's beak; an adjective often used to describe an aristocratic profile.

Archbishop: a bishop of the highest rank who presides over an archbishopric or an archdiocese.

Astrolabe: an instrument that measures the altitude of the sun or other stars, used to solve astronomical and navigational problems.

Autocrat: a person ruling with unlimited authority.

Avant-garde: the unorthodox, daring, or experimental in the literary, visual, or musical arts.

Badinage: playful repartee or banter.

Bailiff: the overseer of a landed farm or estate.

Ballistics: the science or study of the motion of projectiles in flight.

Betrothal: a promise of marriage.

Bolshevik: "majority-ite"; a member of a Russian political party that advocated the immediate and forceful seizure of power.

Bombardier: an artilleryman.

Boudoir: a woman's bedroom or sitting room.

Bow: the forward end of a ship.

Brigade: a large body of troops constituting a military unit.

Brocade: a silk fabric with raised patterns of embroidery, typically in gold and silver.

Caftan: a long, loose garment that has long sleeves and is tied at the waist.

Charlatan: an impostor or fraud; one who feigns knowledge or skills.

Chatelaine: the mistress of a castle.

Chorister: a singer in a choir.

Clairvoyance: the ability to see objects or actions that are imperceptible to the senses.

Colic: acute pain in the abdomen or bowels.

Conscript: to draft for military or naval service; one drafted into such service.

Consort: the husband or wife of a reigning monarch.

Coronation: the act or ceremony of crowning a sovereign.

Corset: a tight undergarment fitted with whalebone or similar material laced to shape and support the body.

Cossacks: people of southern and southwestern Russia descended from Tatar groups, known for their horsemanship; organized into a cavalry in the army of tsarist Russia.

Coup: a sudden and decisive overturn or upset of power.

Courtier: an attendant at a royal court.

Cyrillic: the alphabet used for writing Russian and various other Slavic languages.

Decembrists: members of the unsuccessful revolt against the tsar in December 1825.

Despot: a ruler with absolute, unlimited power.

Distaff: a staff with a cleft end for holding wool or flax from which thread is drawn by hand for spinning.

Dowager: a woman of high social position, usually a widow, and often an owner of a title or property; a dignified elderly woman.

Droshky: a small, open carriage.

Duma: an elected town or city council, responsible for public services such as schools, water, and paving; during the reign of Nicholas II, the principal legislative assembly.

Ecclesiastics: members of the clergy or other individuals in religious orders.

Electress: the wife or widow of an elector, a German prince of the Holy Roman Empire.

Emancipation: the state or act of being freed from any type of bondage to, control by, or power exerted by another.

Enamel: a glassy substance applied to the surface of glass, metal, or pottery by fusion; the coating created serves as decoration or protection.

Enlightenment: philosophical movement of the 18th century that stressed reason over traditional social, political, and religious ideas.

Epaulet: an ornamental shoulder piece, usually worn on military uniforms.

Ermine: a weasel in its winter color of white with a black tip at the tail.

Estate: a piece of landed property, sometimes large, and often including an elaborate house on the grounds.

Farrier: one who shoes horses.

Festoon: to drape and bind fabric at intervals.

Francophilia: the admiration or taste for France or French culture.

Frigate: a naval vessel, usually heavily armed on one or two decks and with an elevated ship rig.

Gentry: the lesser members of the aristocratic class.

Grandee: a man of high social eminence.

Great embassy: a trip taken by Peter I to western Europe to negotiate an alliance against the Turks and to learn modern shipbuilding and navigation.

Great Northern War: a war against Sweden waged by Russia with Poland and Denmark in the early 1700s.

Guarantor: one who gives a guaranty, warrant, or other promise, usually financial.

Hematoma: a swelling caused by a break in a blood vessel.

Hemophilia: a sex-linked genetic disorder in which excessive bleeding occurs because of a deficiency of clotting factors.

Hilt: the handle of a sword or dagger.

Horticulture: the science and art of growing flowers, fruits, and vegetables.

Hull: the frame or body of a ship.

Icon: a religious image, usually painted on small wooden panels and used in the devotions of Orthodox Christians.

Iconostasis: a screen or partition made of wood, stone, or metal, on which icons are placed; in Eastern Christian churches, the iconostasis usually separates the nave from the sanctuary.

Idyll: an idealized pastoral scene.

Impresario: a promoter or manager of a ballet or opera company.

Incendiaries: persons who deliberately set fire to a building or other property.

Kasha: a gruel prepared from hulled and crushed buckwheat groats; a staple food of the Russian peasant.

Khlebosolstvo: "bread-salt"; the Russian word for hospitality.

Kibitka: a large cradlelike carriage or cart on wheels or sled runners in which four people can travel lying down.

Kovsh: a traditional wooden drinking or ladling vessel carved in the shape of a bird.

Kremlin: the citadel of a Russian city. The most famous of the kremlins, in Moscow, houses the central offices of the government as well as a number of palaces and cathedrals.

Kvas: a slightly alcoholic beverage made from fermented rye or barley, having a dark color and a sour taste.

Lapidary: relating to the art of cutting or polishing precious stones.

Libretto: the text of a work for the musical theater.

Lineika: a four-wheeled carriage, sometimes roofed, that can hold as many as eight to 10 individuals.

Litany: a lengthy recitation or enumeration.

Livery: a distinctive uniform, badge, or other type of ornamentation worn by the retainers of persons of rank.

Magnate: an individual of rank, power, or influence.

Menshevik: "minority-ite"; a member of a political party that believed in gradual reform by parliamentary methods.

Mezzanine: a low-ceilinged story between two main stories in a building.

Milliner: a designer, maker, or seller of women's hats.

Millstream: a stream whose flow is used to run a mill.

Muscovy: a Russian principality of the 13th to 18th centuries, centered on its capital of Moscow.

Nagaika: a Cossack whip.

Nakaz: an order or instruction given by the central government to its subordinate officials.

Nave: the principal area of a church; the long, narrow central hall used by the congregation.

Nephrite: a form of jade varying in color from whitish to dark green.

Nobles' Land Bank: a government-sponsored program that provided credit for the gentry as a means of preserving their estates for their descendants.

Orb: a sphere or globe, sometimes bearing a cross; an emblem of sovereignty.

Orthodox Church: the Christian church of eastern Europe and the Near East; the major religion of Russia, in imperial times treated as an arm of the state.

Palisade: a fence of stakes constructed for defense.

Pastor: a clergyman in charge of a local church or parish.

Pastoral: having the charm or serenity associated with rural life.

Patriarch: the head of one of five areas of jurisdiction in the early Christian church.

Pavilion: an open structure used for shelter, concerts, and exhibits.

Pelisse: a long cloaklike garment with slits for one's arms; often lined with fur.

Peredvizhniki: "wanderers"; members of the Society for Traveling Art Exhibitions, a group of artists who toured Russia exhibiting works of art that were often critical of the social order.

Portico: a structure consisting of a roof supported by columns, which is usually attached to a building.

Preobrazhensky Guard: the senior guard infantry regiment in the Imperial Russian Army, formed by Peter the Great.

Principality: a state ruled by a prince.

Proletariat: the working class.

Proscenium: the part of a stage in front of the curtain.

Psalm: a sacred song or poem used in worship.

Queue: to form a line to wait.

Regent: one who governs a kingdom in the absence of the rightful sovereign or during the reign of a minor.

Regime: a government in power or a period of rule.

Regiment: a unit of military ground forces.

Rosette: an arrangement, object, or ornament resembling a rose in shape.

Rowan: a Eurasian tree of the rose family.

Ruble: Russian monetary unit.

Sable: a weasel-like mammal found in cold regions of Eurasia, valued for its dark brown fur.

Samovar: a metal urn with a spigot at its base used in Russia for heating water for tea.

Sarafan: a loose, sleeveless dress worn over a blouse or chemise.

Scabbard: a sheath for a sword or dagger.

Scepter: a rod or baton carried by a sovereign as an emblem of imperial authority.

Scion: a descendant.

Serfs: peasants; individuals bound to the soil and often subject to the will of the landowner.

Slavophile: an adherent of the mid-19th-century Russian philosophy that opposed the westernization of Russia.

Soiree: a social gathering held in the evening.

Sovereign: a king, queen, or other monarch having supreme power.

Steppes: vast level and treeless tracts of land in southeastern Europe or Asia.

Streltsy: "sharpshooters"; established in the 16th century as a personal guard for the tsar and as an elite force in time of war.

Supernumerary: a person not counted among the regulars in a group.

Surrey: a light, four-wheeled pleasure carriage in use beginning in the late 19th century.

Sycophant: a servile or fawning flatterer of one of higher stature.

Table of Ranks: a bureaucratic hierarchy devised by Peter I, which assigned military, court, and civilian service positions on the basis of merit rather than birth.

Teutonic: person of northern European stock; Germanic.

Tiller: farmer or cultivator of soil.

Tricentennial: a 300th anniversary or its celebration; a tricentennial was celebrated on March 6, 1913, in Russia to mark 300 years of Romanov rule.

Tsar: sovereign ruler; a form of the Roman title *caesar*.

Tsarevich: the son of a tsar.

Tsarina: the wife of a tsar; the Russian empress.

Ukase: a decree, order, or proclamation by a Russian emperor or government having the force of law.

Whitsunday: a Christian feast day on the seventh Sunday after Easter; Pentecost.

Zemstvo: a local elected council in which all classes participated, serving as the body of self-governance in rural areas.

PRONUNCIATION GUIDE

Aksakov (ahk-SAH-kof)
Alexander (ah-lek-SAHN-dehr)
Alexandrovich (ah-lek-SAHN-droh-veetch)
Alexei (ah-lek-SAY)
Alkonost (ahl-koh-NOST)
Anastasia (ah-nahs-tah-ZEE-ah)
Anhalt-Zerbst (AHN-halt zehrbst)
Anna (AHN-nah)
Annenhof (AH-nehn-hoff)
Anton Chekhov (AHN-ton CHEH-hof)
Arina Bagrova (ah-REE-nah bah-GROH-vah)
Azov (ah-ZOHF)
Baba Yaga (BAH-bah ya-GAH)
Bagration (bah-grah-TYON)
Bagrovo (Bah-GRO-vuh)
Baratynskaya (bah-rah-TIN-skah-yah)
Barclay de Tolly (bark-LAY de to-LEE)
Berezina (byeh-reh-zee-NAH)
Bolshoi Buguruslan (bohl-SHOI boo-goo-roos-LAHN)
Boris Godunov (bah-REES go-doo-NOF)
Borodin (boh-roh-DEEN)
Borodino (bo-ro-dee-NOH)
César Cui (SAY-sar swee)
Chaliapin (shal-YAH-pin)
Cossack (koh-ZAHK)
Dashkova (dash-KOH-vah)
Diaghilev (DYAH-gee-lef)
Dnieper (DNYEH-pehr)
Dostoyevsky (dah-stoh-YEHV-skee)
Droshky (DROHSH-kee)
Duma (DOO-mah)
Dvina (dvee-NAH)
Ekaterina (yeh-kat-eh-REE-nah)
Elena Dmitrieva (eh-LAY-nah dmee-tree-YEH-vah)
Eudoxia Lopukhina (yehv-doh-KSEE-yah luh-pooh-khee-NAH)
Onegin (uh-NYEH-gin)
Feodor (FYOH-duhr)
Feodorovich (FYOH-duh-ruh-veetch)
Feodorovna (FYOH-duh-ruhv-nah)
Ge (geh)
Georgy Gapon (gee-YOR-gee gah-POHN)
Glinka (GLEEN-kah)
Gogol (GOH-gohl)
Grigory (gree-GOR-ee)
Grisha (GREE-shah)
Hermitage (ehr-mee-TAZH)
Igor Stravinsky (EE-gor strah-VEEN-skee)
Ismailovsky (surname) (is-may-LOHV-skee)
Ismailovsky (park) (is-MAY-lohv-skee)
Ivan (ee-VAHN)

Kalinkina (kah-LEEN-kee-nah)
Karamazov (kah-rah-MAH-zoff)
Kasha (KAH-shah)
Kazan (kah-ZAHN)
Kharkov (HAR-koff)
Khleb (hlyeb)
Khlebosolstvo (hlyebo-SOLS-tvuh)
Khodynka Field (huh-DEEN-kah)
Khristos Voskrese (hree-STOHS voss-KREH-syeh)
Kibitka (kee-BEET-kah)
Knipper (KNEE-pehr)
Konstantin Stanislavsky (kahn-stahn-TEEN stahn-ee-SLAHF-skee)
Kornei Chukovsky (kor-NAY choo-KOHF-skee)
Koshkarov (kahsh-kuh-ROF)
Kovsh (kohfsh)
Kramskoi (krahm-SKOY)
Kursk (koorsk)
Kuskovo (koo-SKOH-vah)
Kustodiev (koo-stoh-DEE-yef)
Kutuzov (koo-TOO-zof)
Kvas (kvahs)
Lenin (LYEH-neen)
Leonid (leh-uh-NEED)
Lineika (lee-NAY-kah)
Litovsky (lee-TOHV-skee)
Livadia (lee-VAH-dyah)
Mariinsky (mah-ree-EEN-skee)
Marius Petipa (MAH-ree-oos peh-tee-PAH)
Maxim Gorky (mak-SEEM GOR-kee)
Menshevik (mehn-sheh-VEEK)
Menshikov (MEHN-sheeh-kof)
Mikhail (mee-HAYL)
Michel Fokine (MEE-shell FOH-keen)
Mily Balakirev (MEE-lee bah-LAH-kee-rehf)
Miloslavsky (mee-luh-SLAHV-skee)
Miloslavskaya (mee-luh-SLAHV-skah-yah)
Modest Mussorgsky (muh-DEHST MOO-sorg-skee)
Monomakh (moh-noh-MAKH)
Nagaika (nah-GAHY-kah)
Nakaz (nah-KAHZ)
Naryshkin (nah-RESH-kin)
Natalya Naryshkina (nah-TAHL-yah nah-RESH-kee-nah)
Nemirovich-Danchenko (neh-mee-ROH-veetch DAHN-chehn-kuh)
Neva (nyeh-VAH)
Nevsky Prospect (NYEHV-skee pruhs-PYEHKT)
Neman (river) (NYEH-mun)
Nikolai (nee-koh-LAHY)
Nikolaievich (nee-koh-LA-yeh-veetch)
Nikolayevna (nee-koh-LAH-yehv-nah)

Nikolenka (nee-KOH-lehn-kah)
Nizhny Novgorod (NEEZH-nee NOHV-guh-rod)
Odessa (oh-DYEH-sah)
Olga (OL-gah)
Orest Kiprensky (ah-REHST kip-REHN-skee)
Orlov (or-LOF)
Ostankino (ah-STAHN-keen-ah)
Pashinka (PAH-shyen-kah)
Pasternak (pahs-tehr-NAHK)
Pavel Tretyakov (PAH-vel tray-tyah-KOF)
Pavlova (PAHV-loh-vah)
Peredvizhniki (pehr-reh-DVEEZH-nih-kee)
Perov (peh-ROF)
Petrograd (peh-truh-GRAHD)
Poltava (pohl-TAH-vah)
Potemkin (po-TYOHM-keen)
Praskovya (prah-SKOHV-yah)
Preobrazhensky (pree-ah-brah-ZHEHN-skee)
Protopopov (pro-toh-POH-pof)
Pskov (pskof)
Pushkin (POOSH-keen)
Pyotr (PYOH-tr)
Radishchev (rah-DEESH-chyef)
Rasputin (rah-SPOO-tin)
Repin (RYEH-peen)
Riga (REE-gah)
Rimsky-Korsakov (REEM-skee KOR-sah-kof)
Rodionovna (ruh-dee-YOH-nov-nah)
Rodzianko (ruh-DZYAHN-kuh)
Romanov (ruh-MAH-nof)
Ropsha (ROHP-shah)
Rostopchin (roh-STOP-chin)
Rus (roos)
Salagova (sah-LAH-goh-vah)
Saltykov (sahl-tee-KOF)
Samovar (sah-moh-VAHR)
Sarafan (sah-rah-FAHN)
Sarov (SAH-rof)
Savva Mamontov (SAH-vah MAH-mon-tof)
Sazonov (sah-ZOH-nof)
Semonovsky (seh-myoh-NOHF-skee)
Sergei (sehr-GAY)
Sergeyevich (sehr-GEH-yeh-veetch)
Shchepkin (shch-YEHP-keen)
Shcherbenin (shchehr-beh-NEEN)
Sheremetev (shehr-eh-MET-yev)
Shibanov (sheeh-BAH-nof)
Shipov (SHEE-pof)
Shvibzik (SHVEEB-zik)
Skavronsky (skah-VROHN-skee)
Smolensk (smuh-LENSK)
Smolny (SMOHL-nee)

Sofia (SOH-fee-ah)
Sophia Augusta Fredericka (SOH-fee-ah AHV-goos-tah freh-deh-REEK-ah)
Sol (sohl)
Spasskoe (SPASS-ko-yeh)
Spiridon (spee-ree-DOHN)
Standart (stahn-DAHRT)
Stasov (STAH-sof)
Stepan Mikhailovich Bagrov (styeh-PAHN mee-HAYL-oh-veetch bah-GROF)
Stepanovich (styeh-PAH-noh-veetch) or (styeh-pah-NOH-veetch)
Stolypin (stoh-LEE-peen)
Streltsy (strehlt-SEE)
Surikov (SOOR-ee-kof)
Suzdal (SOOZ-dahl)

Tamara Platonovna Karsavina (tah-MAH-rah plah-TUH-nov-nah kar-SAH-vee-nah)
Tatiana (tah-TYAH-nah)
Tchaikovsky (chahy-KOHV-skee)
Terem (TEH-rehm)
Tolstoy (tol-STOY)
Troitskoe (TROY-tsko-yeh)
Tsar-Batyushka (TSAHR BAH-tyoosh-kah)
Tsarskoe Selo (TSAHR-sko-yeh syeh-LOH)
Tula (TOO-lah)
Turgenev (toor-GYEH-nyef)
Ufa (oo-FAH)
Ukase (oo-KAHZ)
Valentin Serov (vah-lehn-TEEN seh-ROF)
Vanya (VAHN-yah)
Vasily (vah-SEE-lee)

Vaslav Nijinsky (VAH-slahf nih-ZHEEN-skee)
Vladimir (vlah-DEE-meer)
Volinsky (vuh-LEEN-skee)
Volkonsky (vol-KOHN-skee)
Voronezh (vuh-RUH-nyezh)
Vorontsov (vuh-runt-SOF)
Vyacheslav Plehve (vyah-cheh-SLAHV pleh-VYEH)
Witte (VIT-teh)
Yasnaya Polyana (YAHSS-nah-yah pol-YAH-nah)
Shuvalova (shooh-VAH-loh-vah)
Yuri Dolgoruky (YOO-ree dol-guh-ROO-kee)
Yusupov (yoo-SOO-pof)
Zemstvo (ZEHMST-vuh)

ACKNOWLEGMENTS

The editors wish to thank the following individuals and institutions for their valuable assistance in the preparation of this volume:

American Friends of the Russian Country Estate, Washington, D.C.; Bildarchiv Preussischer Kulturbesitz, Berlin: Heidrun Klein; Borodino Museum, Moscow: Irina Alexeevna Nikolaeva; Central State Archives of Cinematic & Photographic Documents, St. Petersburg: Alexandra Alexandrovna Golovina, S. Ya. Dudko; Tatiana Vasilievna Fedoseyev, Arlington, Virginia; Hermitage Museum, St. Petersburg: Mikhail Borisovich Piotrovsky, Vladimir Matveyev, Anastasia Miklyaeva; Lenin State Library, Moscow: Svetlana Nikolaevna Artamonava; Museum of Ostankino, Moscow: Gennady Viktorovich Volovin, Irina Anatolievna Saprunova; Russian Ethnography Museum, St. Petersburg: Igor Vasilievich Dubov, Alexander Afanasievich Mirin; Russian Museum, St. Petersburg: Evgenia Nikolaevna Petrova, Timofei Germanovich Alexandrov; Russian State Archive of Film and Photographic Documents, Krasnogorsk: Lyudmila Petrovna Zapryagaeva, Mrs. Bolshakova; John F. Sloan, Springfield, Virginia; State Archives of the Russian Federation, Moscow: Sergei Vladimirovich Mironenko, Yelena Chirkova; State Historical Museum, Moscow: Alexander Ivanovich Shkurko, Tatiana Timofeyeva, Vladimir Makarovich Boiko; State Museum of Theater and Music, St. Petersburg: Natalia Ivanovna Metelitsa; Tretyakov Gallery, Moscow: Valentin Alexeevich Rodionov, Lyudmila Mikhailovna, Olyona Yevgenievna Rezchikova.

BIBLIOGRAPHY

BOOKS

Afanas'ev, Aleksandr. *Russian Fairy Tales.* Ed. and trans. by Norbert Guterman. New York: Pantheon Books, 1945.

Alexander, John T. *Catherine the Great: Life and Legend.* New York: Oxford University Press, 1989.

Bird, Alan. *A History of Russian Painting.* Boston: G. K. Hall, 1987.

Brewster, Hugh. *Anastasia's Album.* New York: Madison Press, 1996.

Brumfield, William Craft. *Gold in Azure: One Thousand Years of Russian Architecture.* Boston: David R. Godine, 1983.

The Cambridge Encyclopedia of Russia and the Former Soviet Union. Ed. by Archie Brown et al. New York: Cambridge University Press, 1994.

Cantacuzène, Princess (Countess Spèransky, née Grant). *My Life Here and There.* New York: Charles Scribner's Sons, 1921.

Carmichael, Joel. *An Illustrated History of Russia.* Ed. by Georges and Rosamond Bernier. New York: Reynal, 1960.

Courcel, Martine de. *Tolstoy: The Ultimate Reconciliation.* Trans. by Peter Levi. New York: Charles Scribner's Sons, 1988.

Cracraft, James. *The Petrine Revolution in Russian Architecture.* Chicago: University of Chicago Press, 1988.

Cronin, Vincent. *Catherine: Empress of All the Russias.* London: Harvill Press, 1978.

Daniloff, Nicholas. *Two Lives, One Russia.* Boston: Houghton Mifflin, 1988.

Dmytryshyn, Basil, ed. *Imperial Russia: A Source Book, 1700-1917.* New York: Holt, Rinehart and Winston, 1967.

Dollinger, Hans. *Rußland: 1200 Jahre in Bildern und Dokumenten.* Munich: C. Bertelsmann, 1977.

Fabergé: A Loan Exhibition for the Benefit of the Cooper-Hewitt Museum, the Smithsonian Institution's National Museum of Design, April 22-May 21, 1983. New York: A La Vieille Russie, 1983.

Fabergé Eggs: Imperial Russian Fantasies. New York: Harry N. Abrams, 1980.

Galitzine, George, Prince. *Imperial Splendour: The Palaces and Monasteries of Old Russia.* London: Viking, 1991.

Gaynor, Elizabeth, and Kari Haavisto. *Russian Houses.* Cologne: Evergreen, 1994.

Gilbert, Martin. *Atlas of Russian History.* New York: Oxford University Press, 1993.

Girard, René. *Resurrection from the Underground: Feodor Dostoevsky.* Ed. and trans. by James G. Williams. New York: Crossroad, 1997.

Golynets, Sergei. *Ivan Bilibin.* New York: Harry N. Abrams, 1982.

Grey, Ian:

Catherine the Great: Autocrat and Empress of All Russia. Philadelphia: J. B. Lippincott, 1962.

The Horizon History of Russia. New York: American Heritage, 1970.

Handbook of Russian Literature. Ed. by Victor Terras. New Haven, Conn.: Yale University Press, 1985.

Hapgood, Isabel F. *Russian Rambles.* New York: Arno Press, 1970.

Haxthausen, August von. *Studies on the Interior of Russia.* Chicago: University of Chicago Press, 1972.

Hilton, Alison. *Russian Folk Art.* Bloomington: Indiana University Press, 1995.

The Horizon Book of the Arts of Russia. New York: American Heritage, 1970.

Hudson, Hugh D., Jr. *The Rise of the Demidov Family and the Russian Iron Industry in the Eighteenth Century.* Newtonville, Mass.: Oriental Research Partners, 1986.

International World Atlas. Maplewood, N.J.: Hammond, 1977.

Iroshnikov, Mikhail P., Yury B. Shelayev, and Liudmila A. Protsai:

Before the Revolution: St. Petersburg in Photographs, 1890-1914. Trans. by Evgueni Filippov. New York: Harry N. Abrams, 1991.

The Sunset of the Romanov Dynasty. Moscow: Terra, 1992.

Katharina Die Grosse. Kassel, Germany: Staatliche Museen Kassel und Wintershall AG, 1997.

Killens, John Oliver. *Great Black Russian: A Novel on the Life and Times of Alexander Pushkin.* Detroit: Wayne State University Press, 1989.

Klyuchevsky, Vasili. *Peter the Great.* Trans. by Liliana Archibald. London: Macmillan, 1958.

Lincoln, W. Bruce. *Between Heaven and Hell: The Story of a Thousand Years of Artistic Life in Russia.* New York: Viking, 1998.

Lyons, Marvin. *Russia: In Original Photographs, 1860-1920.* Ed. by Andrew Wheatcroft. New York: Charles Scribner's Sons, 1977.

Maclean, Fitzroy. *Holy Russia: A Historical Companion to European Russia.* New York: Atheneum, 1979.

Martin, John Stuart, ed. *A Picture History of Russia.* New York: Crown, 1968.

Massie, Robert K.:

Nicholas and Alexandra. New York: Laurel, 1967.

Peter the Great: His Life and World. New York: Ballantine Books, 1980.

Massie, Suzanne. *Land of the Firebird.* New York: Touchstone, 1980.

Mazour, Anatole G. *Women in Exile: Wives of the Decembrists.* Tallahassee, Fla.: Diplomatic Press, 1975.

Milner-Gulland, Robin, and Nikolai Dejevsky. *The Cultural Atlas of Russia and the Soviet Union.* New York: Facts On File, 1989.

Moscow: Treasures and Traditions. Washington, D.C.: Smithsonian Institution, 1990.

Moynahan, Brian. *The Russian Century.* London: Chatto & Windus, 1994.

National Geographic Atlas of the World. Washington, D.C.: National Geographic Society, 1970.

Nicholas and Alexandra: The Family Albums. London: Tauris Parke Books, 1992.

Onassis, Jacqueline, ed. *In the Russian Style.* New York: Viking Press, 1976.

Opolovnikov, Alexander, and Yelena Opolovnikova. *The Wooden Architecture of Russia: Houses, Fortifications, Churches.* Ed. by David Buxton. New York: Harry N. Abrams, 1989.

Palmer, Francis H. E. *Russian Life in Town and Country.* New York: Arno Press, 1970 (reprint of 1901 edition).

Pipes, Richard. *Russia under the Old Regime.* New York: Charles Scribner's Sons, 1974.

Pronin, Alexander, and Barbara Pronin. *Russian Folk Arts.* New York: A. S. Barnes, 1975.

Pushkin, Alexandr Sergeyevitch. *The Complete Prose Tales of Alexandr Sergeyevitch Pushkin.* Trans. by Gillon R. Aitken. New York: W. W. Norton, 1966.

Radzinsky, Edvard. *The Last Tsar: The Life and Death of Nicholas II.* Trans. by Marian Schwartz. New York: Doubleday, 1992.

Riasanovsky, Nicholas V. *A History of Russia.* New York: Oxford University Press, 1984.

Rodimzeva, Irina, Nikolai Rachmanov, and Alfons Raimann. *The Kremlin and Its Treasures.* New York: Rizzoli, 1987.

Roosevelt, Priscilla. *Life on the Russian Country Estate: A Social and Cultural History.* New Haven: Yale University Press, 1995.

St. Petersburg: A Travellers' Companion. Comp. by Laurence Kelly. London: Constable, 1981.

Sanders, Jonathan. *Russia 1917: The Unpublished Revolution.* New York: Abbeville Press, 1989.

Sarabianov, Dmitri V. *Russian Art: From Neoclassicism to the Avant-Garde, 1800-1917.* New York: Harry N. Abrams, 1990.

Senelick, Laurence. *Serf Actor: The Life and Art of Mikhail Shchepkin.* Westport, Conn.: Greenwood Press, 1984.

Seroff, Victor I. *The Mighty Five: The Cradle of Russian National Music.* New York: Allen, Towne &

Heath, 1948.

Serov, Valentin Aleksandrovich. *Valentin Serov: Paintings, Graphic Works, Stage Designs.* New York: Harry N. Abrams, 1982.

Shvidkovsky, Dmitri. *St. Petersburg: Architecture of the Tsars.* Trans. by John Goodman. New York: Abbeville Press, 1996.

Smakov, Gennady. *The Great Russian Dancers.* New York: Alfred A. Knopf, 1984.

Sokolov, Y. M. *Russian Folklore.* Trans. by Catherine Ruth Smith. Detroit: Folklore Associates, 1971.

Solodkoff, Alexander von. *Masterpieces from the House of Fabergé.* New York: Harry N. Abrams, 1989.

Sutherland, Christine. *The Princess of Siberia: The Story of Maria Volkonsky and the Decembrist Exiles.* New York: Farrar Straus Giroux, 1984.

The Times Atlas of the World. New York: Times Books, 1980.

The Times Atlas of World History. Ed. by Geoffrey Barraclough. Maplewood, N.J.: Hammond, 1993.

Townend, Carol. *Royal Russia.* New York: St. Martin's Press, 1995.

Troyat, Henri:
Catherine the Great. Trans. by Joan Pinkham. New York: Meridian, 1994.
Divided Soul: The Life of Gogol. Trans. by Nancy Amphoux. Garden City, N.Y.: Doubleday, 1973.
Peter the Great. Trans. by Joan Pinkham. New York: E. P. Dutton, 1987.

Valkenier, Elizabeth Kridl. *Ilya Repin and the World of Russian Art.* New York: Columbia University Press, 1990.

Vyrubova, Anna. *The Romanov Family Album.* New York: Vendome Press, 1982.

Wallace, Robert, and the Editors of Time-Life Books. *Rise of Russia* (Great Ages of Man series). Alexandria, Virginia: Time-Life Books, 1967.

Wiley, Roland John. *Tchaikovsky's Ballets: Swan Lake, Sleeping Beauty, Nutcracker.* Oxford, England: Clarendon Press, 1985.

Wilmot, Martha. *The Russian Journals of Martha and Catherine Wilmot.* London: Macmillan, 1934.

Worrall, Nick. *The Moscow Art Theatre.* London: Routledge, 1996.

PERIODICALS

Daniloff, Ruth. "How Czar Nicholas Was Outfoxed by the Guardian Angels." *Smithsonian,* June 1991.

OTHER SOURCES

Goldsmith to the Imperial Court of Russia: Fabergé, 1846-1920. Exhibition catalog. London: Victoria and Albert Museum, 1977.

Ilyin, Olga. "The Court and I: A Memoir." Unpublished memoir, n.d. Courtesy Boris Ilyin.

Snowman, A. Kenneth. *The Art of Carl Fabergé.* Boston: Victoria and Albert Museum, 1977.

INDEX

Time-Life Books is a division of Time Life Inc.

TIME LIFE INC.
PRESIDENT and CEO: George Artandi

TIME-LIFE BOOKS
PRESIDENT: Stephen R. Frary
PUBLISHER/MANAGING EDITOR: Neil Kagan
VICE PRESIDENT, MARKETING: Joseph A. Kuna

What Life Was Like
IN THE TIME OF WAR AND PEACE

EDITOR: Denise Dersin
DIRECTOR, NEW PRODUCT DEVELOPMENT:
Elizabeth D. Ward
DIRECTOR OF MARKETING: Pamela R. Farrell

Deputy Editor: Paula York-Soderlund
Design Director: Cynthia T. Richardson
Text Editor: Robin Currie
Associate Editor/Research and Writing:
Trudy W. Pearson
Senior Copyeditors: Mary Beth Oelkers-Keegan, Anne Farr
Technical Art Specialist: John Drummond
Picture Coordinator: David Herod
Editorial Assistant: Christine Higgins

Special Contributors: Charlotte Anker, Ronald H. Bailey,
George Daniels, Ellen Galford (chapter text); Jane
Coughran, Sarah L. Evans, Mimi Harrison, Christina
Huth, Marilyn Murphy Terrell (research-writing);
Meghan K. Blute, Jessica K. Ferrell, Stephen M. Graves,
Beth Levin (research); Dale Brown, Janet Cave (editing);
Barbara L. Klein (index and overread); Ann Lee Bruen
(copyediting).

Correspondents: Maria Vincenza Aloisi (Paris), Christine
Hinze (London), Christina Lieberman (New York). Valu-
able assistance was also provided by Angelika Lemmer
(Bonn), Loretta Martin (Moscow). Special thanks to
Vlada Kuznetsova, Andrei Strelkov, Andrei Polikanov,
Oleg Nikishin, Eduard Basiliya (Moscow).

Director of Finance: Christopher Hearing
Directors of Book Production: Marjann Caldwell,
Patricia Pascale
Director of Publishing Technology: Betsi McGrath
Director of Photography and Research: John Conrad Weiser
Director of Editorial Administration: Barbara Levitt
Production Manager: Gertraude Schaefer
Quality Assurance Manager: James King
Chief Librarian: Louise D. Forstall

Consultant:
Priscilla Roosevelt, author of *Life on the Russian Country
Estate,* is a fellow of the Institute for European, Russian,
and Eurasian Studies at George Washington University.
Also the author of *Apostle of Russian Liberalism: Timofei
Granovsky,* a monograph on Leo Tolstoy, and numerous
articles on Imperial Russian culture, she has served as
president of the Southern Conference on Slavic Studies
and on various panels and committees of the American
Association for the Advancement of Slavic Studies. Profes-
sor Roosevelt recently became a member of the steering
committe for Russia's A. S. Pushkin Bicentennial, which
will be celebrated in 1999.

Library of Congress Cataloging-in-Publication Data
What life was like in the time of war and peace :
Imperial Russia, AD 1696-1917 / by the editors of Time-
Life Books, Alexandria, Virginia.
          p.   cm.—(What life was like ; 10)
     Includes bibliographical references and index.
     ISBN 0-7835-5459-1
     1. Russia—History—1689-1801. 2. Russia—
History—1801-1917.
I. Time-Life Books. II. Series: What life was like series ; 10.
DK131.W48 1998   98-37820
947—dc21   CIP

Other Publications:
HISTORY
Our American Century
World War II
The American Story
Voices of the Civil War
The American Indians
Lost Civilizations
Mysteries of the Unknown
Time Frame
The Civil War
Cultural Atlas

COOKING
Weight Watchers® Smart Choice Recipe Collection
Great Taste~Low Fat
Williams-Sonoma Kitchen Library

SCIENCE/NATURE
Voyage Through the Universe

DO IT YOURSELF
Total Golf
How to Fix It
The Time-Life Complete Gardener
Home Repair and Improvement
The Art of Woodworking

TIME-LIFE KIDS
Student Library
Library of First Questions and Answers
A Child's First Library of Learning
I Love Math
Nature Company Discoveries
Understanding Science & Nature

For information on and a full description of any of the
Time-Life Books series listed above, please call 1-800-
621-7026 or write:

Reader Information
Time-Life Customer Service
P.O. Box C-32068
Richmond, Virginia 23261-2068

This volume is one in a series on world history that
uses contemporary art, artifacts, and personal accounts
to create an intimate portrait of daily life in the past.

Other volumes included in the
What Life Was Like series:

On the Banks of the Nile: Egypt, 3050-30 BC
In the Age of Chivalry: Medieval Europe, AD 800-1500
When Rome Ruled the World: The Roman Empire, 100 BC-AD 200
At the Dawn of Democracy: Classical Athens, 525-322 BC
When Longships Sailed: Vikings, AD 800-1100
Among Druids and High Kings: Celtic Ireland, AD 400-1200
In the Realm of Elizabeth: England, AD 1533-1603
Amid Splendor and Intrigue: Byzantine Empire, AD 330-1453
In the Land of the Dragon: Imperial China, AD 960-1368